WELCOME
GREAT AIR BATTLES OF WORLD WAR TWO

Great Air Battles of World War Two? The word means 'great' in terms of scale and importance, it isn't a glorification of war. Within the following pages we recall the heroism – during success and failure – from some of the most critical aerial confrontations of the European and Pacific combat theatres from 1939-1945. Here you will find action from the RAF's first desperate and ultimately disastrous air raid skirmishes, followed by the Battle of Britain's literally 'hardest day.' Moving to the Mediterranean theatre we study the heroic defence of Malta. I am sure many if you will know of the story of *Faith*, *Hope*, and *Charity*, the three legendary Gloster Gladiators said to have led Malta's aerial defence...but could their 'fame' be better described as 'fable'? See inside...

Japan's shock 1941 attack upon Pearl Harbor brought the Unites States, somewhat unprepared, into what was now a truly World War. The US learned a bitter lesson as its Marine pilots were forced to fly obsolete aircraft in combat, often at the cost of their lives, yet they ultimately emerged triumphant in the battle for Midway Island in the battle that changed the course of the Pacific war.

Despite the magnitude of the aforementioned battles, the many mass combats that raged in the day and night skies of Europe were certainly the numerically largest the world has ever seen. By day, and often without Allied fighter support, the American B-17s and B-24s, flying at the edge of their performance, slugged it out with Luftwaffe fighters day after day while the Royal Air Force night bombing campaign kept the pressure up 'around the clock'. The combats associated with Allied bomber strikes against Regensberg, Schweinfurt, and Nuremberg will forever be remembered when people discuss courage in combat.

These desperate battles involved the most famous Allied and Axis fighters and bomber aircraft of World War Two and this publication serves as a tribute to those who took part. Lest we forget.

Tom Allett
Editor

BELOW: B-17Gs of the USAAF's 384th Bomb Group on a bomb run, 1944. USAF

CONTENTS

6 The Battle of the Heligoland Bight
It was a disaster for the RAF – a formation of unescorted Vickers Wellingtons flying over the North Sea to target German warships was devastated by German fighters. Steve Beebee reflects on a battle that changed RAF strategy in World War Two.

14 The Hardest Day
On August 18, 1940, the Luftwaffe mounted three huge bombing raids on Britain. The strength of the resistance and the sound defensive tactics were more than it had bargained for, resulting in significant losses for both sides. Steve Beebee looks back at the Battle of Britain's 'Hardest Day'.

22 RAF Aircraft
Profiles of some of the key aircraft serving the Royal Air Force during World War Two.

24 The Malta Gladiators
Everyone knows the legend of the three Gloster Sea Gladiators, named *Faith*, *Hope*, and *Charity*, which held the line in Malta during World War Two. Matthew Willis uncovers the real story behind them.

34 Pearl Harbor
In terms of influencing the course of World War Two, few air actions can have had the dramatic effect of Japan's surprise attack on Pearl Harbor in December, 1941. Thomas Cleaver looks back on that fateful event.

44 US Aircraft
Colour artwork of some of the historic aircraft operated by the USAAF and US Navy during the battles retold in this publication.

46 Massacre of Marines at Midway
Andy Thomas explains that within the US forces' crucial victory at the Battle of Midway was a punishing blow against the US Marine Corp's Brewster Buffalo squadrons.

54 Japanese Navy Aircraft
Andy Hay's artwork brings detail to some of the aircraft in use by the Japanese Imperial Navy in the war for control of the Pacific.

56 Dogfights over Dieppe
Operation Jubilee was a costly defeat for the Allies that went on to pay dividends two years later. Andy Thomas explains how lessons learned at Dieppe paved the way for the successes of D-Day.

66 Regensburg and Schweinfurt: Deep penetration disaster
Needing to crush Messerschmitt fighter production, US bomber crews fought a savage gun battle high over Germany. Tom Allett tells their sobering story.

74 Luftwaffe Aircraft
Nazi Germany developed some of the best-known aircraft of World War Two and these colour profiles by Andy Hay puts them in focus.

76 One hell of an Argument
The sheer scale and ferocity of Operation Argument, an all-out attack on Germany's aircraft production capabilities, led it to be remembered as 'Big week'. Tom Allett recalls the events of February 20 to 25, 1944.

82 Nuremberg Nightmare
It was meant to be Bomber Command's big sign-off before switching focus to the Allied preparations for D-Day. But, as Tom Allett tells, the operation led to more men lost in a single night than Fighter Command had lost during the entire Battle of Britain

90 The most critical 24 hours
The D-Day invasion of Normandy was arguably the most crucial day of the war on the western front. Allied air power had played a major role in preparing the way for the amphibious assault upon the Normandy beaches. Ken Delve investigates how effective were the efforts on the day of the invasion?

98 Surprise Attack
Operation Bodenplatte, the Luftwaffe's desperate attempt to regain air superiority in western Europe, ended in defeat. Thomas Cleaver recounts what was probably the wildest fight ever for a USAAF Eighth Air Force fighter unit.

106 Black Friday
Jamie Ewan explains why February 9, 1945, was the darkest of days for the Royal Air Force's Coastal Command when it was tasked with finding and sinking the *Z-33*.

Star of the UK airshow circuit, Duxford-based B-17G *Sally B*, uses smoke generators to replicate battle damage. KEY-STEVE FLETCHER

ISBN: 978 1 83632 000 5
Editor: Tom Allett
Senior editor, specials: Roger Mortimer
Email: roger.mortimer@keypublishing.com
Cover Design: Steve Donovan
Design: SJmagic DESIGN SERVICES, India
Advertising Sales Manager: Sam Clark
Email: sam.clark@keypublishing.com
Tel: 01780 755131
Advertising Production: Becky Antoniades
Email: Rebecca.antoniades@keypublishing.com

SUBSCRIPTION/MAIL ORDER
Key Publishing Ltd, PO Box 300, Stamford, Lincs, PE9 1NA
Tel: 01780 480404
Subscriptions email: subs@keypublishing.com
Mail Order email: orders@keypublishing.com
Website: www.keypublishing.com/shop

PUBLISHING
Group CEO and Publisher: Adrian Cox

Published by
Key Publishing Ltd, PO Box 100, Stamford, Lincs, PE9 1XQ
Tel: 01780 755131 **Website:** www.keypublishing.com

PRINTING
Precision Colour Printing Ltd, Haldane, Halesfield 1, Telford, Shropshire. TF7 4QQ

DISTRIBUTION
Seymour Distribution Ltd, 2 Poultry Avenue, London, EC1A 9PU
Enquiries Line: 02074 294000.

We are unable to guarantee the bona fides of any of our advertisers. Readers are strongly recommended to take their own precautions before parting with any information or item of value, including, but not limited to money, manuscripts, photographs, or personal information in response to any advertisements within this publication.

© Key Publishing Ltd 2024
All rights reserved. No part of this magazine may be reproduced or transmitted in any form by any means, electronic or mechanical, including photocopying, recording or by any information storage and retrieval system, without prior permission in writing from the copyright owner. Multiple copying of the contents of the magazine without prior written approval is not permitted.

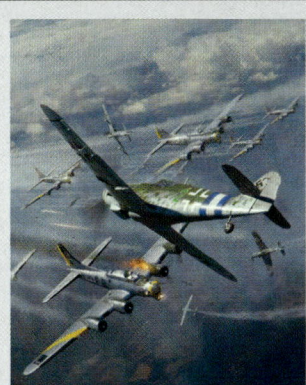

FRONT COVER IMAGE:
Luftwaffe Messerschmitt 109s of fighter units JG300 and JG301 charge into a close formation of B-17s from the 390th Bomb Group. The B-17s were heading for Magdeburg in northern Germany, during the huge Allied air offensive of January 1945.
PIOTR FORKASIEWICZ WWW.PETERFOR.COM

HELIGOLAND BIGHT

THE BATTLE OF THE HELIGOLAND BIGHT

It was a disaster for the RAF – a formation of unescorted Vickers Wellingtons flying over the North Sea to target German warships was devastated by German fighters. We reflect on a battle that changed RAF strategy in World War Two

WORDS: STEVE BEEBEE

The Battle of the Heligoland Bight, fought on December 18, 1939, was not only one of the first air battles of World War Two, but it's considered to be the first 'named battle' of the conflict. It involved Vickers Wellingtons of the Royal Air Force (RAF) flown into action against the German Kriegsmarine (navy), the considerable assets of which were vigorously defended by Luftwaffe fighters. The events took place at a time when the British clung to the soon to be outdated belief that well organised flights of bombers would be largely invulnerable to fighter intervention.

It was therefore a serious and sharp lesson in the dangers of unescorted, daylight bombing.

The Heligoland Bight is part of the North Sea off the northwest coast of Germany, near the Heligoland archipelago. It's also the area close to the port of Wilhelmshaven where several key German Kriegsmarine warships were harboured, notably the battlecruisers *Scharnhorst* and *Gneisenau*, both seen as immensely significant to – and even symbolic of – the German war effort.

The RAF leadership was aware of the value of these and other such assets in the area, and the menace facing British shipping both from these vessels and U-boats was all too clear. The RAF's aim at this early stage of World War Two was to disrupt German shipping routes and naval operations by targeting these warships and other naval vessels. It hoped to avoid bombing the German mainland. December 18, 1939, marked the first major daylight raid by the RAF on German assets, the beginning of a gradual shift towards a more aggressive bombing campaign against the enemy.

The sortie that day involved a force of 22 Wellington bombers – originally 24, with two turning

BELOW:
Frank Petts' Wellington Mk.Ia N2873 WS-P, after landing at Sutton Bridge following the disastrous Heligoland mission.
J PETTS VIA A GOODRUM

6 GREAT AIR BATTLES OF WORLD WAR TWO

www.key.aero

ABOVE: On its first raid on September 4, 1939, 9 Squadron flew the Wellington Mk.I that lacked power operated turrets but flew in the tight formations that persisted until December. 9 Sqn Records. ALL VIA ANDREW THOMAS

back before the action began. The aircraft that participated came from three RAF units, Nos 9, 37 and 149 Squadrons. The air crews had been told that enemy fighter action posed minimal threat to bomber formations, but the majority had been given little training in maintaining a rigorous formation, let alone in the face of enemy fire.

The RAF had hoped that a daylight raid in clear weather would catch the Germans off guard, especially given that the enemy's radar detection systems, and indeed co-operation between naval and air forces, were not as sophisticated or entrenched as its own. The British consequently put faith in a notion that now seems naïve – that anti-aircraft defences and fighter response would be minimal.

Unsurprisingly, given the clear conditions and the raid's proximity to German fighter airfields, the unescorted bombers were met with heavy resistance from the defenders. As the Wellingtons flew over the area of their target, they were intercepted by a significant number of Luftwaffe fighters. Intense air-to-air combat ensued. The Wellingtons were met by a mixture of Luftwaffe Messerschmitt Bf 109s and Bf 110s, a total of 44 aircraft. Elements from Jagdgeschwader (fighter wing) 1 (JG 1), JG 26, and Zerstörergeschwader ('heavy fighter' or destroyer wing) 76 (ZG 76) were all involved in what turned out to be a costly day for the RAF and its mostly inexperienced crews.

The German fighters, using superior tactics and experience, inflicted heavy losses on the bombers, which were unable to maintain formation in the fray. Of the 22 bombers that took off, 12 were shot down and several others were damaged. The Germans lost only three fighters, and only two due to enemy fire.

Taking on the warships

During the so-called Phoney War, the period immediately after Britain's declaration of war on Germany, the main threat to British interests was the U-boat. The submarines immediately began to target vessels bringing in supplies from North America and other parts of the British Empire, with U-47 also

RIGHT: Sgt Frank Petts (second from left) and his 9 Squadron crew after the Heligoland sortie of December 18, 1939. L-r: Sgt Lawson, Petts, LAC Whitham and LAC Balsh. J PETTS VIA A GOODRUM

HELIGOLAND BIGHT

RIGHT: Fg Off Bill McRae's Wellington with its wings and fuselage shredded by enemy fire after reaching the sanctuary of North Coates. VIA M J F BOWYER

sinking the battleship HMS *Royal Oak* in October 1939, with the loss of 786 crew. German shipping therefore became the RAF's primary target.

With the Netherlands and Belgium seeking to remain neutral, RAF bombers were not permitted to fly over, and nor were they allowed to operate from bases in France for fear of retaliation. Bombers therefore had to fly east over the North Sea towards Denmark before turning south towards the Heligoland Bight where concentrations of German naval power could often be located.

A reconnaissance flight on September 3, 1939, by a 139 Squadron Bristol Blenheim reported a large Kriegsmarine force off Wilhelmshaven. A task force comprising 15 Handley Page Hampdens and nine Wellingtons was despatched, but poor weather prevented them from locating any targets. Further attempts were made in the following days, but with poor results. Although a 9 Squadron raid did engage German warship *Admiral Scheer* and the light cruiser *Emden*, seven RAF aircraft failed to return. The German Freya radar, though not as sophisticated as its British equivalent, did give the Luftwaffe some notice of the raid, and three pilots from JG 77 claimed 'kills' – these are likely to have been the first RAF aircraft shot down by enemy fighters in the war.

So inexperienced were RAF crews at this point in the war – a factor that would become painfully clear during the Battle of the Heligoland Bight – that one Wellington mistook the Danish town of Esbjerg for the German port of Brunsbüttel, some 150 miles to the south, and dropped bombs on it.

Although the RAF did have some success in the coming weeks, with the German vessel *Brummer* and a minesweeper sunk in a strike by Wellingtons of 149, 38, and 115 Squadrons, British losses remained high. Five of the twin-engined bombers were shot down on December 14 – all of which were claimed by German fighters. Ominously, the RAF refused to believe that the quintet had been brought down by fighters and thus maintained faith in the idea that tight formation flying was the key to self-defence.

German forces were themselves going through changes. Attempts were made, without initial success, to create a greater understanding between the different forces – land, sea, and air. Matters were not helped by poor relations between the Luftwaffe and Kriegsmarine commanders-in-chief, Hermann Göring and Erich Raeder. Oberst Carl-August Schumacher, a former leader of II./JG 77 who had served with the German navy during World War One, was given command of fighter units defending Germany's north coast. It was hoped that his naval experience would lead to better co-operation, but in

BELOW: 149 Squadron crews after the Heligoland Bight raid on December 18, 1939. P H T GREEN COLLECTION

reality, Schumacher and his naval equivalent were of the same rank, meaning there was no direct chain of command.

Despite this frustration, Schumacher had numerous aircraft – a mixture of Bf 109s and Bf 110s – at his command, and they could be despatched to defend Wilhelmshaven and the surrounding area very swiftly, from Schillig, just 15 miles to the north.

Meanwhile, the RAF had hastily set up No.3 Group, comprising six squadrons with two in reserve, to undertake daylight missions. Heligoland Bight, and the Kriegsmarine, were to be their targets in a raid mounted by 9, 37, and 149 squadrons. Given that it had been set up for night bombing, this decision was dubious as was the quality of the training. Only two of the units within No.3 Group, 214 and 9 squadrons, had received sufficient tuition in this skill. Mock combats

> **It was the first major daylight raid by the RAF on German assets, the beginning of a gradual shift towards a more aggressive bombing campaign against the enemy**

with Supermarine Spitfires that suggested the formations would be decimated were ignored. With the 'pocket battleship' *Admiral Graf Spee* being scuttled in Uruguay that month after sustaining serious damage in the Battle of the River Plate, there was a strong appetite in the British military to see more German armour sunk.

Wg Cdr Richard Kellett and Sqn Ldr Paul Harris of 149 Squadron were the only experienced combat leaders, but they had no chance to practice formation flying with all the crews that would be involved in the Heligoland sortie. For the mission, slated for December 18, they would be airborne without sufficient training or clear tactical advice about what to do if engaged by fighters. While the mission was to be flown in broad daylight, and in fine weather, in

 **DON'T MISS OUT ON OTHER KEY AVIATION MAGAZINE SPECIALS**
If you'd like to be kept informed about Key Publishing's aviation books, magazine specials, subscription offers and the latest product releases. **Scan here »**

HELIGOLAND BIGHT

ABOVE: A rarely seen image of a Wellington Mk.Ia of 9 Squadron with its ventral turret deployed.
T MASON VIA C BOWYER

one sense its crews could not have been more in the dark.

Into the fray

The attacking force comprised 24 aircraft, less the two that would turn back, and they set out in four formations of six, the first led by Wg Cdr Kellett. Taking off from RAF Mildenhall in Suffolk just before 0930hrs, Kellett was the first to leave the ground, while aircraft from 9 Squadron lifted off from RAF Honington. Before heading out over the North Sea the aircraft formed up over King's Lynn. With other machines from 37 Squadron taking off from Feltwell, the idea was to form up in a unit before passing over the east coast, but the latter unit did not catch up with the main body of aircraft until later.

The first three 'boxes' of six, drawn from 149 and 9 squadrons, were each composed of two 'vics' in line astern. No. 37 Squadron's sextet brought up the rear, but these flew in three pairs in line astern formation. The plan was to fly well to the north of their intended destination, in a bid to avoid heavy anti-aircraft fire from installations on the Frisian Islands. The day was clear and sunny – the aircraft would be highly visible and vulnerable to ground fire if they strayed too near to enemy territory.

Before the formation was ready to turn south towards the Heligoland Bight it lost the pair. Wellington N2984, flown by Flt Lt Duguid, had to abandon the sortie due to engine trouble – it was escorted home by N2398 – and the remaining bombers continued east before making a turn to the south, homing in on their target in perfect visibility.

The formation had intentionally flown further to the east than strictly necessary – the idea was to fly over the harbour not from the north, from which direction the defenders might be anticipating an enemy strike, but effectively through the 'back door'. Kellett led his aircraft towards the north German city of Schleswig, flying south before turning west towards the target. In terms of surprise, the move was effective as no German aircraft were airborne to meet them. The Freya radar had picked up the incoming formation, but poor communication

ABOVE: Wellington Mk.Ia OJ-J of 149 Squadron was shot down over the Frisian Islands, probably during one of the raids in late 1939. J-L ROBA

LEFT: Wellington Mk.Ia OJ-E of 149 Squadron at Mildenhall three days after the Heligoland raid. P H T GREEN COLLECTION

lines resulted in a delayed reaction. Maj Harry von Bülow-Bothkamp of II./JG 77 later put the blame on the navy, as it was their radar that picked up the raiders. It did mean that the Wellingtons approached their target without aerial intervention, though flying in perfect visibility they were at once bombarded by a variety of potent ground fire.

For Carl-August Schumacher, the notion of a British raid on such a day seemed far-fetched. On that morning, a Freya set was being demonstrated to a visiting naval officer on the island of Wangerooge, and to the surprise of its operator, Lt Hermann Diehl, it clearly picked up a signal from the north as the Wellingtons approached. However, when contacting Schumacher's wing, he was told that nothing had been heard from the 'official' naval radar operators, and that the very idea of the British attacking in such clear skies seemed absurd. Even when the Kriegsmarine radar did pick up the Wellingtons, nothing was done for 20 minutes so poor was the line of communication. Only when observers noted the approach of the RAF raid were fighters scrambled to meet them.

> **The day was clear and sunny – the aircraft would be highly visible and vulnerable to ground fire if they strayed too near to enemy territory**

Shot out of the sky

As the Wellington formation approached its target, overflying Cuxhaven on the German north coast, it came under heavy fire from three flak positions. Kellett turned west, now heading over the estuary and towards Wilhelmshaven. Their target now certain, five more anti-aircraft batteries fired upon them, accompanied by a barrage from vessels in the dock, including *Scharnhorst* and *Gneisenau*. The Wellingtons suddenly faced mighty opposition, and with fighters now lifting off to intercept them, things were about to get a lot worse.

The Germans had been briefed to attack Wellingtons from the side (beam) as this was considered a blind spot for RAF gunners. Also, because the Vickers twins lacked self-sealing fuel tanks, fire was likely to rip through the wings if hit. Attacking from the stern was easier, but considered too dangerous as it gave defending gunners a clear target. Adding to the dangers for the RAF crews was the doctrine instilled into them that fighters were of minimal concern to well managed bomber formations. Even though German fighters were spotted lifting off from Schillig to the north, the bombers pressed on.

It is thought that only 149 Squadron actually dropped bombs on ships at Wilhelmshaven harbour – just six 500lb (230kg) bombs fell, and it's not known if they caused any damage. As the Wellingtons emerged from this relatively inconsequential bomb run, the formation had started to become dispersed. Bringing up the rear, 37 Squadron had fallen behind, while Sqn Ldr Archibald Guthrie, leading the machines ▶

HELIGOLAND BIGHT

from 9 Squadron, had moved too far ahead of the other five. Similarly, in a bid to bring his 37 Squadron machines back in line, Sqn Ldr Ian Hue-Williams increased his speed but struggled to keep his own formation together.

As the flak bombardment ceased at approximately 1330hrs, the enemy fighters pounced. While overclaiming was rife (the Germans claimed 38 'kills', considerably more than the 22 bombers participating), there is no doubt that the Wellingtons were decimated, a total of 12 failing to return home. The first 'kill' was credited to Utfz Heolmayr, while Oblt Johannes Steinhoff, flying a JG 26 Bf 109D, claimed two. Ten minutes later, Hptm Wolfgang Falck led Bf 110s from ZG 76 into the fray, claiming four Wellingtons destroyed. With his aircraft seriously damaged by return fire, Falck managed to glide back to base and was able to land safely.

Less fortunate was Oblt Johann Fuhrmann who, having failed to hit Sqn Ldr Paul Harris's 149 Squadron machine in the suggested beam attack, switched his attentions to another aircraft, from the stern, and was hit by return fire. His fighter crippled, Fuhrmann ditched into the sea not far from the island of Spiekeroog but drowned while attempting to swim to safety.

Both Guthrie and Hue-Williams' aircraft were lost in the attack. Possibly singled out as targets because they had not maintained a tight formation with their flight, Guthrie's Wellington fell to the guns of Bf 110 pilot Oblt Gordon Gollob, while Hue-Williams' aircraft N2904 was last seen with the starboard wing burning furiously and heading out to sea off Wilhelmshaven. He and his crew are commemorated on the Runnymede Memorial at Egham, near Windsor.

Elsewhere, the claims continued to mount. Utfz Fresia believed he had shot down two of the RAF machines, the second of which was that piloted by Fg Off Douglas Allison, another now remembered at Runnymede. The Germans suffered

ABOVE:
A Wellington of 149 Squadron being loaded with 500lb GP bombs.
P H T GREEN COLLECTION

LEFT:
Wellington Mk.Ia crews of 149 Squadron at Mildenhall preparing for a raid, possibly that of December 18.
P H T GREEN COLLECTION

ABOVE:
Wg Cdr Richard Kellet, OC of 149 Squadron led the December raid. He's pictured at Mildenhall in January 1940. VIA ANDREW THOMAS

a second casualty when Lt Roman Stiegler crashed into the sea while pursuing Fg Off Lemon's Wellington, but several more bombers were claimed, five by ZG 76 Bf 110 pilots.

Schumacher was credited with the destruction of Fg Off Peter Wimberley's 37 Squadron aircraft, N2888, although it also took hits from Helmut Lent. Wimberley was the sole survivor and spent the rest of the war as a prisoner. Like 'Macky' Steinhoff, Lent would go on to become a highly regarded 'ace', though unlike Steinhoff he did not survive the war. As well as firing on N2888, Lent is believed to have accounted for Sgt Herbie Ruse's aircraft, N2936, as well as Fg Off Arthur Thompson's 37 Squadron machine. The latter crashed just off the coast of Borkum. Another 37 Squadron machine, that of Plt Off Oliver Lewis, was also shot down nearby, falling to the guns of Schumacher.

After around 20 minutes of intense action, the German aircraft began to return to their bases. It had been an incredibly costly afternoon for the three RAF units involved. Only ten of the 22 Wellingtons that made it to the target returned home, and the majority landed with some damage from the onslaught they had endured. Sgt Frank Petts managed to land his 9 Squadron machine at Sutton Bridge while Fg Off Bill McRae brought his heavily damaged aircraft into North Coates, both in Lincolnshire. The raid had been a failure, the losses extreme and probably hard to comprehend for the survivors. Certainly, the results served to decimate Bomber Command's illusions surrounding unescorted daylight bombing.

A harsh lesson

Above all else, the battle highlighted the vulnerability of unescorted bombers in daylight raids, leading to changes in RAF tactics. While the Luftwaffe's success boosted German morale, the heavy losses for the RAF were a sobering experience, leading to a re-evaluation of their overall bombing strategy.

The raid was undeniably a failure for the RAF. The heavy losses underscored the vulnerability of bombers operating without fighter escort during daylight missions. The one-sided battle could even be regarded as a turning point in air warfare, as it so clearly demonstrated the dangers of daylight bombing. The lessons learned influenced future Allied bombing strategies, ultimately leading to the development of long-range fighter escorts and more co-ordinated air operations. After December 1939, the RAF began to focus more on night bombing raids to reduce losses.

The Battle of the Heligoland Bight highlighted the challenges of early World War Two air combat and demonstrated the importance of air superiority and tactical innovation. It was a sobering experience for the RAF, shaping their strategic approach for the rest of the war and illustrating the evolving nature of aerial warfare. ■

> ❝ The Wellingtons suddenly faced mighty opposition, and with fighters now lifting off to intercept them, things were about to get a lot worse ❞

RIGHT:
This Wellington, possibly N2936 LF-J of 37 Squadron, was downed at Borkum on December 18, 1939. J-L ROBA

THE HARDEST DAY

THE HARDE

On August 18, 1940, the Luftwaffe mounted three huge bombing raids on Britain. The strength of the resistance and the sound defensive tactics were more than it had bargained for, resulting in significant losses for both sides. We look back at the Battle of Britain's 'Hardest Day'

WORDS: STEVE BEEBEE

Battle of Britain Day is marked annually on September 15, commemorating the epic day on which the Luftwaffe threw its might at London, only to be met with reciprocal determination from a far from decimated Royal Air Force. While nobody could doubt the significance of that date, it was nevertheless almost a month earlier, on August 18, 1940, that saw the campaign's hardest fought day. Over time that date has become known, simply, as The Hardest Day.

While September 15 has come to be seen as a turning point in the crucial battle for control of British skies, the results of The Hardest Day are more challenging to interpret. Both the Luftwaffe and the RAF lost a similar number of aircraft. What is more certain is that the former did not achieve its intended results. This was not through lack of courage or airmanship, but more through vagaries of weather and, more than anything, a largely well organised response from the RAF, aided by radar.

While outnumbered by the Luftwaffe, the notion that the defenders were weakened and demoralised, or close to defeat, proved untrue on either of these significant dates. This came as an unwelcome surprise to the invaders and was, ultimately, their undoing.

Preparing for 'Sea Lion'

Following victories in their military campaigns across Western Europe and Scandinavia, Germany hoped that Britain would not wish to continue the fight. When surrender was not forthcoming, the aggressors' hopes switched to knocking out British air defences. Superiority in the air was considered the least it had to achieve in order to mount Unternehmen Seelöwe (Operation Sea Lion), the mooted invasion of the United Kingdom.

ST DAY

ABOVE:
A view of Hawker Hurricane Mk.I P2923 at Castle Camps. Flt Lt 'Dickie' Lee was missing in action flying this aircraft on August 18, 1940. 85 SQN RECORDS

A crossing of the Channel was considered highly dangerous due to British naval strength – an air campaign was therefore the chosen option.

Although June 1940 had seen the Battle of France ending in German victory, the Luftwaffe needed time to regroup and bolster its depleted forces. While it did target British shipping and occasionally airfields during July, it had to wait until August before a full-strength attack could be mounted.

Although the bombardment of convoys was not as successful as hoped, it certainly caused disruption, prompting Britain to redirect much of its shipping to northeastern shores. With those targets largely removed, and more aircraft arriving at Luftwaffe bases in northern France, Germany turned its attention to British airfields. The idea was to destroy the bulk of British air defences on the ground, in the hope that this would prompt surrender or, as a last resort, make a seaborne invasion more viable.

By August 12, the Luftwaffe was escalating its attacks – and while they certainly achieved some success, it was not as great as hoped, or believed. On the 13th, a day nicknamed Adlertag (Eagle Day), the Luftwaffe made

> **Radar stations, filter rooms and plotters feeding intelligence to fighter controllers meant British forces had ample warning of incoming attacks**

THE HARDEST DAY

RIGHT: Plt Off Albert G Lewis lands 85 Squadron Hurricane Mk.I P2923 VY-R at Castle Camps in Cambridgeshire on July 25, 1940. It was later flown by 'Dickie' Lee. 85 SQN RECORDS – ALL IMAGES VIA ANDREW THOMAS

BELOW: Flt Lt Carl Davis of 601 Squadron led the unit's 'Red' section on the afternoon of August 18. VIA T HOLMES

its heaviest assault on the RAF to date, committing over 70% of its bomber force and more than 80% of its Messerschmitt Bf 109 and Bf 110 fighters and fighter-bombers. Due to poor intelligence, this and subsequent raids did not achieve the devastating impact the aggressors had hoped for.

The same poor intelligence gave rise to the belief that, by August 17, the RAF was down to its last 300 serviceable fighters. Even though the RAF was significantly outnumbered in terms of overall aircraft, the true figure was around the 850 mark, with others in storage or at training units. The Luftwaffe would be in for an unpleasant surprise when they undertook their three main attacks on August 18, The Hardest Day.

On the 18th, the Luftwaffe planned to target RAF Sector Stations. It was decided to focus on those at Kenley, North Weald, Hornchurch, and Biggin Hill, with a separate attack – led by Junkers Ju 87 dive-bombers – aiming to strike at coastal bases and the RAF's 'eyes and ears' - its radar network. Albert Kesselring, the commander of Luftlotte 2, set about destroying key RAF airfields by sending in large numbers of bombers escorted by mostly single-engined fighters, plus other fighters given more of a 'free chase' role. Rather than going after numerous targets at once, Kesselring decided to concentrate his efforts on a shortlist. Crews were briefed on secondary targets in the event of main objectives being unreachable for any reason, but the key strategy was to hit important targets with maximum strength.

During the Battle of France, RAF fighters had mostly operated in unnecessarily tight and unwieldy formations, often meaning pilots were more concerned with not colliding with one another than engaging the enemy. This was in stark contrast to the far more flexible Rotte and Schwarm formations adopted by Luftwaffe fighters – effectively a 'finger four', this meant all involved could keep an eye out for threats while being free to make attacks from advantageous positions. By August 1940, the RAF had greatly improved its tactics, though they still lacked the flexibility enjoyed by their opponents.

The RAF did, however, have immensely sophisticated defences by the standards of the day. The network of radar stations, filter rooms and plotters feeding intelligence to fighter controllers meant British forces had ample warning of incoming attacks, and at least some idea of the numbers involved. Crucially, this meant that the bulk of their assets could get airborne, or positioned to the best strategic advantage, before the Luftwaffe had the opportunity to destroy them on the ground or otherwise press home its intended attack.

Two-pronged attack

The first Luftwaffe wave on that significant day was directed to attack Biggin Hill and Kenley. Kampfgeschwader (KG) 1, equipped with 60 Heinkel He 111s, was briefed to perform a high-altitude raid on the former, while KG 76 flying a total of 48 Dornier Do 17s and Junkers Ju 88s was directed to hit Kenley. Five Jagdgeschwader (JG, fighter wings), some 150 aircraft, were to operate in support of these operations, along with the Bf 110s of Zerstörergeschwader (ZG) 26, a 'destroyer' or 'heavy fighter' wing. Ideally, the fighters would fulfil both close escort and free-hunting roles.

Of the two operations, the one involving KG 76 was the more complex. It involved aircraft striking Kenley in three waves. Ju 88s were expected to open proceedings,

> **A massive air battle commenced – stretching 25 miles from Gosport to Bognor Regis, it was likely an incredible sight**

dive-bombing airfield hangars and other buildings from high altitude, while minutes later Dorniers would follow this up by bombing runways. Finally, nine Do 17s from 9 Staffel (squadron) would fly in at very low level to hit targets of opportunity. The latter tactic had worked extremely well in France, and while flying at wave top or treetop level came with obvious hazards, it had the advantage of eluding radar.

All seemed sound in theory, but weather and poor co-ordination were to make things considerably more difficult – and less effective.

In the event, rather than arriving last on the scene, to 'finish off' a devastated airfield, 9 Staffel was in fact the first to get there. While its presence had not been picked up on radar, it had certainly been noted and even fired upon by Royal Navy boats and observer corps posts. The two larger, higher altitude formations were the subject of radar plots, and as the picture became clearer, RAF fighter units launched in strength to meet the incursion. As 9 Staffel arrived over Kenley it was bombarded by intense ground fire and dived upon by Hawker Hurricanes of 111 Squadron.

The Staffel did hit several buildings, including at least three hangars, but every one of its aircraft was hit in return. Two Hurricanes were shot down, but four Dorniers were lost, with the other five limping home. One of those that made it home was flown by Oblt Hermann Magin – grievously wounded, he died shortly after returning. His navigator, Obfw Wilhelm-Friedrich Illg, had taken the controls and assisted Magin in bringing the Do 17 home, for which act he was later awarded the Knight's Cross of the Iron Cross.

As the Ju 88s arrived over Kenley they saw it already shrouded in smoke from 9 Staffel's attack, making the planned dive-bombing raid impractical. The bombers and their escorting fighters were swiftly engaged by Hurricanes and Supermarine Spitfires, as well as becoming the focus for concentrated ground fire. One of the invaders quickly fell to 32 Squadron's Plt Off Boleslaw Wlasnowoski. Faced with an impossible situation, the Germans instead began dive-bombing their alternate target, West Malling, as their escort was tied up battling elements of four RAF fighter units.

Meanwhile, the Heinkels of KG 1 had had a relatively clear run to their target. Four of the five

ABOVE: Sgt Herbert J L 'Darky' Hallowes attacked several Ju 87s over West Sussex on August 18. P H T GREEN COLLECTION

BELOW: Hans-Joachim Kastner's Messerschmitt Bf 110C 3U+EP was downed near Newchurch on the day. VIA J WEAL

THE HARDEST DAY

ABOVE: British flying ace Flt Lt Derek Boitel-Gill of 152 Squadron shot down a Ju 87 off Bournemouth on August 18. He died in a flying accident the following year. VIA C F SHORES

RIGHT: Plt Off 'Dutch' Hugo of 615 Squadron was wounded in an August 18 combat and treated at a hospital in Orpington. VIA C F SHORES

BELOW: 501 Squadron Hurricane Mk.I P3059 SD-N (Plt Off Ken Lee) and P3208 SD-T (Plt Off R C Dafforn) depart Hawkinge on August 15. Both aircraft were shot down three days later. 501 SQN ASSOC

airborne RAF squadrons were countering the Kenley incursion, giving the watchful Germans the impression that the defenders were down to their last few aircraft. This commonly held belief was to have serious repercussions for the Luftwaffe later in the campaign. The relatively few defending fighters (from 610 Squadron) that met the formation were effectively tied up by fierce resistance from JG 54's Bf 109s. Only one Heinkel fell, probably to a Spitfire from 65 Squadron that sighted the huge formation while 610's fighters were occupied with JG 54.

As the Germans turned for home, fresh challenges faced both sides. Thickening haze made it more difficult for the RAF fighters to target their quarries, but the Germans had an arguably bigger problem. As more Spitfires and Hurricanes joined the fray, the single-engined Bf 109s were running low on fuel, meaning they were in no position to escort the many stragglers attempting to find safe passage back to France. The haze was probably their best hope, but understanding this, the RAF's 11 Group AOC Keith Park told his fighter pilots to spread out in order to have eyes on as much airspace as possible. Pilots were told they could engage singly if necessary.

In this manner, ZG 26 lost five Bf 110s to 56 Squadron, with more falling to the guns of 54 and 501 squadrons. Sources differ on the precise number of '110s downed, but it marked the beginning of the end for the type in the close escort role. The British forces too had taken serious losses, and airfields had sustained damage, but the Luftwaffe had not achieved the devastating results it had sought.

Stuka strike

It was then the turn of the Luftwaffe's feared dive-bombers to enter the fray. Having caused much carnage and confusion in previous battles, Luftlotte 3 commander Hugo Sperrle hoped his charges could hit installations on the British south coast with equal potency. The targets that afternoon were the radar station at Poling in West Sussex, plus RAF Ford, Thorney Island, and Gosport. However, following an analysis of poor-quality reconnaissance images, the Germans were under the false impression that the three bases were fighter airfields. In fact, RAF Thorney Island was a naval air station hosting two Bristol Blenheim units assigned to Coastal Command, Gosport was home to a torpedo development unit, and Ford was then hosting the Fleet Air Arm's Fairey Albacore-equipped 829 Squadron.

The Junkers Ju 87s of Sturzkampfgeschwader (StG) 77 were given the bulk of the task, with further 'Stukas' from StG 3 allotted the job of destroying facilities at Gosport. This considerable force, comprising around 110 of the distinctive, 'bent-winged' dive-bombers, were supported by an even larger collection of Bf 109 fighters, some 157 in total from four different JG. Of these, JG 2 were to fly a sweep of the area in advance, with JG 53, 32, and 27 operating as close support to the Ju 87s. Each 'Stuka' was loaded with a 550lb bomb under the fuselage along with four 11lb bombs, two under each wing. In order to meet their escort at the optimum time, the relatively ponderous Ju 87s took off well in advance of the Bf 109s.

RAF units were quick to react, as the radar station at Poling picked up the incoming raiders – though it underestimated their numbers. With the Hurricanes of 601 Squadron already airborne, both No.11 and No.10 Groups committed units to the fray. Others were unavailable as they had not long returned from battling the previous incursion. Even with the Blenheims of 235 Squadron taking off, the RAF was outnumbered two to one by the Messerschmitts alone, and four to one overall.

The Ju 87s reached the coast en masse, before splitting into four groups to attack their allocated targets. Their escort had successfully reached them and flew zigzag patterns overhead as the dive-bomber crews entered the fray. The attack on Poling was a success,

ABOVE:
615 Squadron's Hurricane Mk.I KW-F was damaged during the Luftwaffe attack on Kenley. VIA A PRICE

exploding bombs putting it out of action for the rest of the month. LACW Avis Hearn courageously remained at her post at Poling, passing on information, despite the devastation around her. She was awarded the Military Medal the following month.

As Poling was effectively (albeit temporarily) knocked out, even greater damage was done at poorly defended RAF Ford. An enormous blaze broke out, destroying aircraft, hangars, and buildings, with 28 killed. Similar results were recorded at Gosport, though thankfully there were no casualties. Spitfires from 234 Squadron were embroiled in battles with the Bf 109s but were unable to prevent the Ju 87s hitting their targets.

For the 28 attackers tasked with hitting Thorney Island, however, it was a different story. Hurricanes from 43 and 601 squadrons were able to engage the 'Stukas' before the Luftwaffe escort could intervene. Some nevertheless pressed home their attack and much damage was done, but at a very heavy cost to the aggressors. With the Bf 109s now getting involved, a massive air battle comprising some 300 aircraft commenced. Stretching 25 miles from Gosport to Bognor Regis, it was likely an incredible sight to anyone not already taking shelter.

As is often the case in the confusion of warfare, figures for claims and losses are varied. There is, however, no doubt that the Ju 87s suffered badly – ten of the 28 that were aiming for Thorney Island were eliminated and another was damaged beyond repair. Even the other, more successful attackers were countered by fighters after ▶

RIGHT:
Hurricane Mk.I P3757 YO-G was crash-landed on August 18 by Fg Off Hartland de Mintarville. H HALLIDAY

THE HARDEST DAY

LEFT: 501 Squadron pilots at Hawkinge on August 16. Standing l-r: Fg Off S Witorzenk, Flt Lt G Stoney, Sgt F Kozlowski. Sitting l-r: Sgt R Dafforn, Sgt P Farnes, Plt Off Ken Lee, Flt Lt J Gibson, Sgt H Adams. Lee and Kozlowski were shot down by Oblt Gerhard Schöpfel of III./JG 26 on August 18. Dafforn baled out during the action and Stoney was killed in the late afternoon. Both Farnes and Witorzenk made claims during the day. 501 SQN ASSOC

their strikes and suffered losses. The impact was severe, with the Ju 87 taking no further role in the Battle of Britain save for occasional convoy strikes.

For the defenders, while there was no doubt that the attacks had caused serious damage, the Luftwaffe had erred in focusing their firepower on what were, largely, the wrong targets. None of the installations hit were fighter bases, and while radar was an essential tool for the RAF, knocking out only one such site caused little problem in a wider context. Not only was Poling running successfully again within weeks, but a mobile unit on the Isle of Wight provided sufficient cover for it even during its downtime. Although it might be argued that the Luftwaffe had the 'right idea' in trying to take out radar, the reality was that in the 70 miles of coastline around Poling a total of six radar facilities provided cover – the loss of one, especially only for a few weeks, was not significant.

Thwarted raids

In the late afternoon, the Luftwaffe turned its attention to its two other major targets, RAF North Weald and Hornchurch. It fell once again to Luftlotte 2 – and Kesselring – to press these attacks home.

The He 111s of KG 53 were directed to attack North Weald, crossing into England over Foulness, while KG 2's Do 17s headed for Hornchurch via a crossing at Deal. The two formations were to pass over the coast at around the same time, heavily supported by an escort comprising around 140 Bf 109 and Bf 110s from five different geschwader. This time, British estimates on enemy numbers were correct and no fewer than 13 squadrons were scrambled from 11 Group, with orders also passed to the more northerly 12 Group, which had its headquarters at Watnall, Nottinghamshire.

Five 11 Group units were in position and ready to meet the invaders as they passed over Foulness and Deal. As KG 53's Heinkels approached North Weald, the RAF's 56 Squadron Hurricanes attacked them while Spitfires from 54 Squadron attempted to engage the escorts. With the German intention now clear, further RAF

BELOW: A Junkers Ju 86P flew a reconnaissance sortie at high level during the early afternoon of August 18. VIA J-L ROBA

units – totalling more than 60 Hurricanes – joined the fray.

The Heinkel crews faced a yet bigger problem – the weather. With the cloud base falling to just 3,500ft their intended raid from 12,000ft was an impossibility, so at around 1740hrs KG 53 gave up on the idea and turned for home. At this point, they were engaged by numerous Hurricanes making a head on attack, while others closed on their rear. Among the losses was II./KG 53's leader, Maj Reinhold Tamm, whose He 111 fell to the guns of 151 Squadron's Plt Off Richard Milne.

Shortly after, among numerous other engagements, Sqn Ldr Peter Townsend's 85 Squadron Hurricanes fought the Bf 110s of ZG 26, and later accounted for a Heinkel. However, the British unit's Flt Lt Richard 'Dickie' Lee, a nine 'kill' ace, was reported missing in action, last seen pursuing Bf 109s out at sea. The German bombers dumped their bombs, destroying or damaging numerous properties in Shoeburyness.

Meanwhile, KG 2 found the low cloud base similarly frustrating, and their accompanying escort was effectively blocked by Hurricanes from 501 and 32 Squadron. A furious battle between the RAF fighters and Bf 109s ensued, with losses suffered by both sides. Unable to accurately hit Hornchurch and chastened by anti-aircraft fire from the naval yard at Chatham, and from the south bank of the Thames estuary, the Dorniers turned for home. Many still had full bomb loads. Returning over Deal, three took the opportunity to attack a Royal Marines barracks, but to all intents and purposes, the incursions made by both bomber groups had failed. The Hardest Day was over.

ABOVE: At the height of the battle in August 1940, 152 Squadron groundcrew 'take five' at a tented dispersal at Warmwell with Spitfire Mk.I R6763/UM-H behind. M W PAYNE

BELOW: AVM Keith Park was AOC 11 Group on August 18. He's pictured on September 15, 1940, with his personal Hurricane. HQ 11 GP

Mixed fortunes

As was often the case, both sides made exaggerated aerial victory claims. In reality, the losses were similar. Around 70 German aircraft were destroyed, with a similar number of losses for the British, including aircraft hit on the ground. However, less than half of Luftflotte 2 and 3's available aircraft had been committed to the day's action, whereas the RAF was more greatly stretched. Fighter Command had nevertheless managed to fly almost 930 sorties, the Luftwaffe having grossly underestimated its strength.

What is perhaps more significant is that the Germans did not succeed in disabling any of their key targets for a lengthy period, or in some cases at all. While the tactics, targeting key fighter airfields, was sound, they were met with fierce resistance prompted by the early warning afforded by radar. They were further troubled by poor weather, principally low cloud base and haze which made hitting the targets either more difficult or impossible.

Despite the tactically sound drive to bomb airfields, very few RAF fighters were destroyed on the ground due to the force's high state of readiness. While knocking out the radar station at Poling was a sensible idea in principle, and a success at least in the short term, it was not significant enough to cause major problems for the defenders. Attacks on other sites during that wave were misdirected in that the targets were not of key significance to the RAF's main defensive effort.

Overall, losses came at a rate that neither side could afford to sustain for long. Each side suffered more losses on August 18, 1940, than on any other date during the campaign. It is perhaps for this reason, more than any other, that this dramatic day of air combat is rightly thought of and referred to as the Battle of Britain's Hardest Day. ■

RAF AIRCRAFT OF WORLD WAR TWO

Vickers Wellington 1.A N2871 'WS-B' of IX(B) Squadron, RAF Honington, December 1939. This aircraft survived a series of Messerschmitt Bf 109 attacks during a 20-minute running fight during the disastrous 'Battle of Heligoland Bight'. The bomber was heavily damaged, but its crew made a successful emergency landing at RAF North Coates. ALL PROFILES ANDY HAY-FLYINGART

Spitfire Vb AA853 'WX-C' was flown by Wing Commander Stefan Witozenc of the 1st Polish Fighter Wing during Operation Jubilee, the Dieppe Raid, of August 1942. Later transferred to 350 Squadron, this aircraft was lost following a mid-air collision with another Spitfire from the same unit in April 1944.

Hawker Hurricane 1 P2970 'US-X' of 56 Squadron, RAF North Weald. On what became known as the Battle of Britain's 'Hardest Day' – August 12, 1940 – it was hit by return fire during an attack on a Dornier 17. Its pilot, P/O Geoffrey Page, baled out but suffered burns to his hands and face. After treatment as a member of the 'Guinea Pig Club' Page was able to return to operational flying and survived the war.

Gloster Sea Gladiator N5519 'R' *'Charity'* Malta 1942. During the siege of Malta, the story of the three Gladiators, *Faith*, *Hope*, and *Charity* holding off the far stronger Luftwaffe became an enduring legend. Subsequent research has proven the Gladiators' service was more beneficial for morale-boosting purposes than operational use.

DH Mosquito FB.VI NS952 'OM-S' of 107 Squadron, Operation Overlord, June 1944. This unit converted to the 'Wooden Wonder' and night intruder duties in February 1944, remaining in that role until the war's end. NS952 was shot down by flak while attacking a railway station on August 25, 1944. Its pilot, Flt Lt Rippon, was killed but his navigator Flt Sgt Ridout, aided by the Maquis, evaded capture and was able to return to his unit.

SIEGE OF MALTA

THE MALTA GLADIATORS

Everyone knows the legend of the three Gloster Sea Gladiators, named Faith, Hope, and Charity, which held the line in Malta during World War Two. But what's the real story behind them? **WORDS:** MATTHEW WILLIS

On September 3, 1943, Air Vice Marshal Keith Park, hero of the Battles of Britain and Malta, delivered a speech on Palace Square, Valletta. Across from him, in the middle of the square, sat the skeletal remains of an aeroplane. It had no wings, no tyres, and most of its cowling panels were missing. Park, on behalf of the Royal Air Force, was presenting this near-wreck to the people of Malta. He said: "In May 1940, Malta possessed no fighter defences and the AOC obtained from C-in-C Mediterranean four Gladiators belonging to the Fleet Air Arm, which were lying in store at Kalafrana. As there were no fighter pilots in Malta, six RAF pilots volunteered to form a small fighter flight, which was formed at Hal Far on 4 June 1940. Italy declared war on 11 June, and, at 06.45hrs of that day a flight of three Gladiators took off to intercept a formation of 10 Italian bombers that attempted to attack the dockyard and Hal Far aerodrome. The enemy formation was driven off, and, during the evening, the Gladiators were again despatched to intercept a formation of 25 enemy bombers. Three of the Gladiators were christened *Faith*, *Hope* and *Charity*.

For 18 days following the Italian declaration of war, three Gladiators were airborne daily and intercepted a total of 144 Italian bombers and fighter escort. During that period, the Gladiators destroyed or badly damaged five enemy aircraft without loss to themselves and succeeded in turning away many formations of bombers." He introduced the aircraft as *Faith*, one of the first four Malta Gladiators, and concluded: "The defence of Malta can justifiably be included among the epics of this war, and *Faith* has earned a place of honour in the armour of Malta."

Park's speech was summarised in the HMSO booklet *The Air Battle of Malta*, published in early 1944. Both did much to cement the myth

BELOW:
Sea Gladiator N5520 was used in the initial skirmishes over Malta on June 11-12, 1940, flown by Fg Off J. L. Waters. It was later fitted with a Mercury VIII engine and Hamilton propeller from a Blenheim in order to keep it serviceable.
NWMA VIA ANDREW THOMAS

ABOVE: *Faith*, *Hope*, and *Charity* – undoubtedly the most famous of all Gladiators, even if the legend involves a good deal of myth alongside the fact. These three Sea Gladiators of the Hal Far Fighter Flight, photographed in June 1940, are N5520, N5531 and N5519. J PICKERING VIA ANDREW THOMAS

of the Gladiators *Faith*, *Hope*, and *Charity*, but it was a myth already in widespread circulation. Soon afterwards, Gloster used the story in advertising, proudly claiming: "The official record reports that in 'the Battle of Malta' there were available in 1940 four Gloster Gladiators in crates! These, uncrated and assembled, were flown by four flying boat pilots who were complete strangers to fighters! One machine was shot down but the remaining three, christened *Faith*, *Hope* and *Charity*, defended the Island against all that Italy could produce for two long months."

In recent times, the story has been questioned and aspects of it ascribed to wartime myth-making and symbolism. Important questions remain. How did a strategically important site like Malta come to lack fighter defence until a shoestring operation was cobbled together on the eve of war? Did a few obsolete biplanes really hold the line for up to two months? And how did they come by their names? The story has at its heart a kernel of truth, but the facts are more complicated. Indeed, most sources are contradictory. The full truth may never be pinned down with certainty.

Malta was an important site for British forces in the inter-war period due to the dockyard and anchorage it provided for the Royal Navy located between the strategic ports of Gibraltar and Alexandria. Fears over its security grew in the mid-1930s with the Italian invasion of Ethiopia and the international tensions it caused. The island had no fighter defences, and only a handful of anti-aircraft guns. At a time of rearmament, Malta always fell too far down the list of priorities.

In the summer of 1939, the Admiralty was highly concerned and asked the Joint Overseas and Home Defence Committee to examine the matter of its air defences. The committee could reach no agreement and passed the matter to the Committee of Imperial Defence (CID), suggesting two schemes: 'A,' which included 64 AA guns and one fighter squadron, and 'B' with 172 AA guns and four fighter squadrons. In July 1939, the CID decided on scheme 'B' but considered that ministerial approval was needed. Final approval

RIGHT: The Sea Gladiators attached to 806 Squadron in October 1940 prepare for flight from the deck of HMS *Illustrious*, following the launch of the more numerous Fulmars which are visible in the background. The nearest is N5549, while behind are N5513 and an unidentified example. N5549 and N5513 were used to shoot down a Cant Z501 on November 8, the latter being flown by RN ace 'Jackie' Sewell. D J TRIBE VIA ANDREW THOMAS

> **" As there were no fighter pilots in Malta, six RAF pilots volunteered to form a small fighter flight "**

was not received until February 1940, with much of the work "At a low order of priority, when other more important needs had been satisfied."

Throughout the first part of 1940, those conditions were mostly not met. Some progress was made with AA batteries, and a mobile radar unit was provided, but not even a single fighter squadron had been established by April 1940. The lack of infrastructure and personnel was a bar to establishing fighter defences on Malta. It was not enough simply to provide the fighters and their pilots – maintenance personnel, spares, accommodation, and equipment were also required. There were only three airfields on Malta, and they had neither the space nor the facilities to support the planned-for squadrons. And yet something had to be done. Malta, less than 100 miles from enemy airfields, could not go into war with Italy defenceless against air attack. If time were to run out, these shortcomings had to be circumvented somehow. In the spring of 1940, time was running out.

Found fighters

Malta's Air Officer Commanding (AOC) RAF Mediterranean, Air Cdre Forster Maynard, famously decided to take matters into his own hands. There had been fighters on Malta for a year, but not RAF machines, and not for the defence of the ▶

SIEGE OF MALTA

island. A year earlier, on April 30, 1939, 24 Gloster Sea Gladiators in packing cases arrived on SS *Nailsea Court*. Most of these were intended for 802 Squadron, part of HMS *Glorious*' air group, plus a 100% reserve, but six were added as a general reserve for the FAA in the region. Nine of the fighters were assembled and embarked on HMS *Glorious*, the rest remaining crated at Kalafrana. *Glorious* disembarked 802 Squadron in Egypt in October 1939 to go hunting raiders in the Atlantic, the squadron returning to Malta in January 1940 as the carrier returned for a refit at the Malta dockyard. In April, she was about to begin post-refit work-up trials with HMS *Ark Royal* when the invasion of Norway by German forces led to her immediate recall. At this time, 802 Squadron seems to have taken the opportunity to exchange some of its aircraft for unused ones still in storage. The new machines were assembled and test-flown at Hal Far, and the aircraft they replaced presumably struck down and crated up. Nine Sea Gladiators of 802 Squadron embarked on April 11, and the carrier set out for northern waters. It is likely that by this time, Maynard was aware that there were additional Sea Gladiators at Kalafrana. He sought, and gained, approval from the commander-in-chief of the Mediterranean Fleet, Vice-Admiral Andrew Cunningham, to use four of the aircraft for a small fighter flight he intended to form at Hal Far. This left two still in their crates at the seaplane station. The Sea Gladiators were not 'found' or 'discovered' as is often stated, although this framing was used even at the time. They were stored aircraft constituting part of the Fleet Air Arm's fighter reserve for the Mediterranean, and a very slender reserve it was too. In April, six of the crated aircraft were taken up by the Fleet Air Arm to be shipped to Alexandria for HMS *Eagle*, as the small carrier had no fighter defence of its own – 813 Squadron was to operate three Sea Gladiators as a

BELOW: A Sea Gladiator of 806 Squadron crashed on deck aboard HMS *Illustrious* in 1940. This unit contributed to the defence of Malta when *Illustrious* was severely damaged in January 1941.
VIA MATTHEW WILLIS

ABOVE:
RAF Hal Far photographed from the air in May 1941.
VIA MATTHEW WILLIS

and crated, this would have taken place between January and March. The first was apparently ready for a training exercise on April 23. The call for volunteer pilots went out and was immediately answered. The first to join were Flt Lt P. Keeble, Fg Off W. 'Timber' Woods (both formerly with the HQ Flight), Fg Off J. Waters, Flt Lt P. Hartley (both from No.3 AACU), and Flt Lt G. Burges (an aide to Maynard at HQ). There are hints that such a scheme had been dreamt of before it appears in the record – Waters had undergone a week's training with 802 Squadron in early March, and as long ago as December and January, Burges had carried out a few flights on one of the naval squadron's Sea Gladiators. The flight now had four aircraft and six pilots. The story now commonly includes an interlude wherein the Gladiators were ordered back into their crates. Even the HMSO booklet notes, "The training was interrupted once when the aircraft were ordered back into their cases by a higher authority; but the Air Officer Commanding managed to obtain their release again." Some accounts go as far as to suggest that the fighter flight was disbanded, and all the aircraft packed up for shipment to Alexandria. This seems unlikely, as Cunningham had agreed their release and had sought approval to do so from the chief of naval staff. The order, if it happened at all, may have been in error or misinterpreted, as it was at this time that several of the remaining aircraft in storage were shipped out for HMS *Eagle*.

The unit decided on a three-on, three-off rota, with one of the aircraft 'resting' during each operation. Three Gladiators practising interceptions and training with fighter controllers became a familiar sight during May.

The cipher messages

A series of cipher messages on Malta's air defence policy that buzzed between the authorities on Malta and the Air Ministry, the Admiralty and the regional RAF command from May 1940 reveal official thinking about the Gladiators in the crucial days around the opening of hostilities. Far from the stout air defence of legend, the early performance of the Gladiators had the local leaders clamouring for better equipment, insisting that the biplanes were little better than nothing – if ▶

fighter flight. The RAF and the Air Ministry presented the situation as if the aircraft were lying around forgotten, though they would have known this was not the case; in June, the commander-in-chief of RAF Middle East referred to the Malta Gladiators "discovered there in packing cases." Maynard, as AOC Malta, on the other hand, would almost certainly have been aware of the fighters as they were deposited at one of the stations under his command, the seaplane base at Kalafrana. The Hal Far Headquarters Flight had been absorbed into No.3 Anti-Aircraft Co-operation Unit in March. Wg Cdr O'Sullivan took over command of Hal Far from Sqn Ldr Holbrook, who assumed command of No.3 AACU, while Sqn Ldr A. C. 'Jock' Martin was appointed station adjutant. Martin insisted on taking command of the newly minted and entirely unofficial Hal Far Fighter Flight, which 'formed' on April 19 within No.3 AACU. The first four Gladiators to be allocated were N5519, N5520, N5522 and N5531. All but N5522 had previously operated with 802 Squadron, being among the aircraft it exchanged for new ones during *Glorious*' refit, and if they had been disassembled

SIEGE OF MALTA

they were at all. Their perceived inadequacy even briefly persuaded some in the government to call for Malta's complete abandonment as a lost cause. There is a hint that the Gladiators were, at first, not intended to face the enemy at all, and were potentially employed for training purposes, in the expectation that more formal fighter defence arrangements would be in place by the time the shooting started.

On May 4, 1940, a cipher message from Mediterranean HQ to the Air Ministry referred to normal training activities having: "Now ceased but agreement with local civil and air service authorities in order to devote all available resources to practice for local active air defence. These measures include fighter flight of four sea Gladiators taken from Fleet Air Arm Reserve by permission CinC Med and manned by improvised RAF crews now being trained in fighter duties and interception procedure."

This hints that the fighter flight may have initially been established less as a last-ditch defensive measure and more to help train local personnel in the requisite procedures, in the expectation that dedicated fighter resources would arrive before they may be needed. Indeed, it was still days before the invasion of France and the Low Countries, and the realisation that UK might soon fight on alone in the Mediterranean in the event of war.

ABOVE: N5519, known — probably retrospectively — as *Charity*, at Hal Far in 1940. This was one of the initial four aircraft to be assembled for the Hal Far Fighter Flight, and wears FAA S1E colours with roundels and fin flash from June 1940. It has a three-blade Fairey Reed propeller while the Sea Gladiator adjacent has a two-blade Watts prop. KEY COLLECTION

On the day the German army launched Fall Gelb, its assault on the Western Front, the Admiralty sent a message to Cunningham expressing concern about the 'borrowing' of FAA aircraft for Malta's defence. "The use of Sea Gladiators and Swordfish taken from FAA Reserves in Mediterranean for new first line duties manned by RAF must result in corresponding inability to replace casualties or wastage in Fleet Air Arm as shortage of Fleet aircraft is acute and existing commitments already cannot be met. Request your remarks." Swordfish, incidentally, were also acquired for maritime patrol and anti-submarine and surface vessel warfare. Cunningham's response is not recorded, but he was firmly behind the Gladiator scheme and later supported Malta's efforts to build up fighter defence against Air Ministry intransigence.

This was not a petty point on the part of the Admiralty. The question of reserves for carrier-based aircraft was critical. Unlike aircraft on the home front, losses were not easy to replace, and the FAA relied on its in-situ reserves to maintain operational squadrons. The loss of the remaining Sea Gladiators at Kalafrana could have had serious implications for the ability of the FAA's carriers in the theatre to defend themselves against air attack.

Fall Gelb on May 10 threatened to change the picture dramatically. Within a few days, the Allies were hard-pressed on the Western Front as Belgium and the Netherlands fell, and French defences collapsed. By May 19, German forces had pushed the defenders back to the Channel coast. That day, information reached the UK government that Germany might be planning an equally massive assault in the Mediterranean. Unconfirmed sightings of German troop-carrying aircraft were reported in Italy. The following day, the Admiralty noted that the report came from, "An official German source" and added, "Reports a combined German and Italian plan of attack on Balearics, Malta, Gibraltar, Greece, etc."

The British government now believed that it was inevitable that Italy would enter the war, and the only question was when. Preparations began against the possibility of a 'hostile act' committed against Malta by Italy

LEFT: Judging from its condition, this abandoned Sea Gladiator is surely N5520, *Faith*, dumped near Luqa airfield. NWM

28 GREAT AIR BATTLES OF WORLD WAR TWO

before an official declaration of war. This brought the matter of Malta's air defence to critical importance. If there was any question that the Gladiator flight would be required for combat, it was now all but answered. The trouble was the Gladiator flight was causing complications and making it difficult to 'clear the decks' to put Malta on a war footing. The RN suggested the flight of de Havilland Queen Bee pilotless target drones be transferred out of harm's way. Maynard sent a message to Cunningham on May 29, 1940, stating: "Cannot recommend transfer this flight to Egypt under existing conditions here since removal of Queen Bees involves moving marking Swordfish as well and personnel concerned with both now employed on improvised air defence operational duties for provision of Gladiator fighter flight[,] sea reconnaissance and anti-submarine patrols."

The Air Ministry resisted putting further resources into the island's defence but was convinced of the inadequacy of the existing arrangements. On May 30, Wg Cdr N V Moreton, of the flying operations staff, wrote to Albert Durston, the director of operations (naval co-operation) recommending no less than complete withdrawal from Malta. As for the Sea Gladiators, Moreton considered that even they might be more use elsewhere.

"If we go to war with Italy it appears to me to be out of the question to expect the garrison of Malta to do much good with only 4 Sea Gladiators and a few guns", Moreton wrote. "Malta with its puny garrison would probably not be able to hold out for any length of time and in any case can only be regarded as a target for the Italian aircraft. The garrison would probably become a total loss to us eventually and the question is whether the personnel and their equipment would not be more good elsewhere and whether they would not inflict more casualties on the enemy if employed on a less forlorn task. I personally think we ought to abandon Malta and leave booby traps mixed up with all the immovable equipment so that we might not only denied its use to the Italians but might blow up a good many of them with it. The signals suggest there is a Fleet Air Arm reserve of aircraft there. We don't know what that might consist of, but Gladiators would come in handy in Egypt or perhaps in Crete. Do you agree, and if so, do you think it worthwhile sounding the Navy to see whether they would reconsider their desire to hold on to Malta."

Cunningham was no more sanguine about the current state of Malta's air defence, but instead of admitting defeat, he pressed for the island's fighter strength to be bolstered. On June 5, 1940, five days before Italy declared war, he sent an impassioned signal to the Admiralty: "I much regret to add to your anxiety nor do I wish to be unduly alarmist, but I am seriously concerned about Malta in event of war with Italy". He went on, "I am [...] of the opinion that if Malta was heavily bombed and then invaded from the air while Garrison was engaged in dealing with panic and disorder caused among civil population it might well fall without fleet being able to lift a finger to prevent it. I am only too well aware how difficult it would be to spare fighter aircraft for defence of islands but [...] it might well be considered wise to send even one fighter squadron to Malta at expense of some other commitment."

The first sea lord replied: "Your anxiety is fully appreciated. At the moment, with the decisive battle on the Western Front, now in progress, the fighter aircraft available cannot meet the immediate requirements."

'Too fast for Gladiators'

On the evening of June 10, Italy declared war on the UK and France. Fears of a 'sneak attack' proved unfounded, but even with warning, there was little Malta's forces could do to fully prepare. The next morning the first air raids took place on Malta. The Gladiator pilots threw themselves into their forlorn task, but it was immediately apparent that the fighters were too few and, more importantly, too slow. Malta's solitary radar unit detected a raid inbound just before 07.00hrs on June 11. Thirty Savoia-Marchetti SM79s were on their way to bomb Hal Far, with a second wave of 15 of the bombers aiming for the dockyard and a further ten going for Kalafrana. The three fighter ▶

> **The Sea Gladiators were not 'found' or 'discovered' as is often stated, although this framing was used even at the time**

BELOW: A Sea Gladiator in Egypt circa 1942, alongside a Blackburn Roc target tug. This is probably one of the aircraft shipped to Alexandria for HMS *Eagle*'s Fighter Flight in April 1940, and by now used only for second-line purposes.
VIA MATTHEW WILLIS

SIEGE OF MALTA

pilots on duty were Sqn Ldr Martin, Flt Lt Burges and Fg Off Woods. The Gladiators were still climbing when the bombers were overhead their targets. Burges saw a formation of SM79s turning back for Sicily and was able to cut the corner, diving on the last as it passed. He reported scoring some hits, but the aircraft betrayed no damage and soon drew out of range.

Eight raids took place that day, though only the last of the succeeding attacks was on the same scale as the first. The Gladiator pilots did what they could, but several of the raids went unopposed. In the last raid of the day, Woods got into a dogfight with an escorting Macchi MC200 – each claimed the other shot down, while in fact little damage was done to either aircraft – and one bomber was attacked, again with little result.

After the first combats, Burges reported his findings to Maynard, noting: "As soon as I opened up, the Italians poured on the coal and the Gladiator just could not catch up with them." Maynard promised he would see if more speed could be extracted from the biplanes. Away from his pilots, however, Maynard appeared convinced that the Gladiators were simply inadequate. Malta needed Hurricanes.

In fact, HQ Malta had been informed that five Hurricanes would be staging through the island on their way to Egypt on July 13. The day after the first raids, the weather was cloudy, and no air attacks could be made. The brief respite gave the AOC time to make an impassioned plea to the Air Ministry to let him hold onto the Hurricanes. Maynard wrote: "Operations here on June one [sic] showed that [Savoia-Marchetti] S.81 too fast for Gladiators. Although interceptions effected and one EA [enemy aircraft] shot down by Gladiators, only short fleeting attacks possible with this type of fighter. Request you consider the possibility of allotting the five Hurricanes now Tunis to Malta in view of lack of defence here and probability of early successes against Italian aircraft which if obtained likely to have considerable and immediate deterrent and moral effect. Have seven pilots here efficient on Gladiator and fighter drill and procedure. Consider these fully capable after short practice of operating Hurricanes."

Malta's governor, Sir William Dobbie, weighed in: "Raids here yesterday show importance of fighter aircraft. The four Gladiators here though successful in bringing one plane down are too slow... Believe a few effective fighters would have a far-reaching deterrent effect and produce very encouraging results." In fact, the Gladiators had not even scored the single kill they were thought to have made. The damage from the raids was relatively minor, compared with what was to come, but the Gladiator flight had not been able to prevent 11 deaths as well as six army and six navy personnel killed, with 130 people injured, and numerous civilian buildings damaged.

As well as Maynard and Dobbie, Admiral Cunningham and the commander-in-chief of RAF Middle East, Sir Arthur Longmore, begged the Air Ministry to let the Hurricanes stay on Malta. The War Office and the Air Ministry were implacable in their denial. "Your position fully realised but regret that with resources available it is impossible for fighter aircraft to be allotted," was the terse reply from the War Office on June 12.

The Air Ministry now insisted that the Gladiators should be adequate. It signalled, "Fully appreciate your request for Hurricanes but defence of Fleet at Alexandria and in Egypt must take the first priority. Hurricanes must therefore proceed to Egypt. With only four Gladiators your results are most encouraging and confirm our experience here and in Norway that Gladiators even though slower have proved a match for German Bombers faster than the S.81." Perhaps here some confusion arose from the misidentification of the SM79s that had carried out the raids with the far slower SM81.

Maynard tried again at 2200 that night. "Whatever experience elsewhere results here show that Sea Gladiator is markedly inferior in performance to Italian bomber types encountered and paucity of numbers is such that even this limited effort will soon exhaust itself. Apart from vital importance of modern fighter aircraft as element of fortress defence [,] morale of Maltese civilian population is bound to deteriorate

ABOVE:
A scene that has been described as showing the remains of a Sea Gladiator, formerly operated by the Hal Far Fighter Flight and then No.261 Squadron, RAF, sitting on the airfield at Ta'Qali with Hurricane I W9133 of No.261 Squadron in the background. However, it seems it was actually taken at Mersa Matruh, Egypt.
IWM MH 8300

unless far greater success over enemy bombers can be obtained than is the case so far." Civilian morale was uppermost in the minds of Dobbie and Maynard after the raids of June 11. Many of those living near the dockyard had abandoned their homes and crammed the roads leading into the countryside. While the next two years of the siege would show the Maltese population to be unusually resilient, the first day definitely rang alarm bells.

On June 13 only nuisance raids took place, individual bombers appearing sporadically and unloading their bombs before attempting to scurry away before interception. The Gladiators managed to catch one, Fg Off Waters piloting N5520 claiming it shot down, but in reality, it escaped with little damage.

At around midday, two of the expected Hurricanes landed at Luqa, accompanied by a Hudson, but after a brief rest they took off for Mersa Matruh in Egypt. Seeing the modern fighters come and then go undoubtedly prompted disappointment to many on the island, potentially exacerbating the morale difficulties the local authorities were so concerned about. The following day, Dobbie wrote to Cunningham asking for his support in requesting better fighters. "Malta has had numerous bombing attacks in the last few days, and numerous civilian casualties caused." He confided his concerns that civilian morale would not hold up for long, saying: "a few modern fighters here would give much greater reassurance to the population. They would probably destroy some enemy aircraft and act as effective deterrent to attack. This is borne out by unwillingness of enemy to face even our slow Gladiators." Longmore was technically in charge of aircraft deployment in the Middle East and Mediterranean, but thus far had been kept out of the loop and overruled. On June 15, he attempted to clarify matters. "I am not at all clear as to Air Ministry policy regarding fighter defence at Malta," he wrote. "Position seems to be that Malta had no authorised Fighter defence but has shown initiative and enterprise in improvising a flight of inferior performance Sea Gladiators which were discovered there in packing cases and the success achieved by these Gladiators against one or two Italian bombers presumably influenced AOC to ask for the allotment of five Hurricanes en route Egypt… I firmly believe that in this initial phase of the war with Italy if Malta were given even six high performance fighters results out of all proportion could be achieved against irresolute enemy formations and most important also would encourage Maltese population to endure."

There were to be no Hurricanes yet, but two more Gladiators, N5524 and N5529, were unpacked and assembled. The pilots elected to wait on stand-by in the cockpit rather than waiting on deckchairs – Burges considered that the time gained was worth 2,000 vital feet of altitude by the time the enemy bombers arrived. Occasional interceptions were made on June 14-15, though the Gladiators still failed to destroy or even seriously damage any Axis aircraft. The pressure on Malta eased slightly over the next week as Italian bombers concentrated on targets in French Tunisia in retaliation for raids on Sicily.

The bombers returned on June 20 when the floating dock was sunk in Grand Harbour. While taking off to intercept a raid the following day, Sqn Ldr Martin crashed and wrote off N5522, though he was unhurt, and later that day the same fate befell Hartley in N5524. The station engineers rebuilt the latter from the wrecks of both Gladiators, so the flight would gain one fighter back in time, but it was a sobering episode. There were no more Gladiators to be had. On the day war broke out, Moreton had noted: "Confirmed by Cdr Stanley Robinson that there are no other FAA aircraft in reserve at Malta." The Air Ministry had little choice but to allow Malta's defences to be boosted with a few Hurricanes, and the next handful that had been intended for Egypt were permitted to stay. France surrendered on June 22, but this blow was softened somewhat by the delivery, finally, of Hurricanes – two had arrived from Bizerta the day before, and four more that day – while the Gladiators claimed a scalp. Burges, in N5519, with Woods effected a successful interception of a single SM79 from the 216a Squadriglia conducting a reconnaissance flight in the afternoon. The bomber caught fire "Right over Sliema and Valletta," according to Burges, "and caused quite a stir." Burges followed up his success by downing an MC200 on the 23rd, though Woods damaged N5531 on landing.

Malta's leaders still worried. Earnest British efforts on June 24 and 27 to persuade French naval forces in North African ports to disarm failed. Dobbie signalled the War Office on June 29, warning: "The French developments, especially in North Africa, have naturally brought Malta into greater prominence and increased attention from Italy may result… At present I have only four Hurricanes and two Gladiators and latter are fast wearing out." However, far from being a drain on the morale of the people of Malta as Dobbie feared, the Gladiators were having the opposite effect.

Sharing the glory

Much of the attention given to the Gladiators focuses on that time when they alone were the defenders of Malta. However, they remained in the fighter defences for considerably longer, operating alongside Hurricanes – the last was not retired from front-line duties until mid-1941.

Within a couple of days of the first Hurricane arrival there were eight of the monoplane fighters ▶

SIEGE OF MALTA

> **"** *Malta, less than 100 miles from enemy airfields, could not go into war with Italy defenceless against air attack* **"**

on Malta. This was considered to be more than the island needed, and with Egypt still considered vulnerable, three flew off on June 24. The surviving Sea Gladiators were therefore still important to the defence of the island, even given the lack of confidence in them expressed by the AOC, the governor, and the Air Ministry. The biplanes held the line solely until the beginning of July, when the locally based pilots were sufficiently trained on the Hurricane to carry out operational flights with them. The biplanes continued to fly out against air raids, and along with the Hurricanes the occasional kill was achieved, delighting the civilian population whenever an enemy aircraft was brought down on the island. For the first ten or 11 days of July, most if not all fighter sorties were carried out with Hurricanes, but as the inevitable damage and wear asserted itself, the Gladiators were brought back into action. N5524 took part in an interception in Burges's hands on July 12, alongside a Hurricane.

Burges had by now been credited with three aerial victories and three probables, some of them scored with the Gladiator and others with Hurricanes, and the day after his latest the *Times of Malta* announced he had been awarded the Distinguished Flying Cross. The newspaper coverage was a hit with the population and Burges's photograph was soon to be seen all over the island. Although Burges was flying both types at the time, his fame seems to have become particularly associated with the Gladiator. Indeed, by July 17, the Hurricanes were mostly unserviceable, and the burden of fighter defence once again fell chiefly to the biplanes. Gladiators took part in interceptions for the final five days of the month, culminating on July 31, when the first of them was shot down.

While there had been fighter escorts from the first day of raids, these had become stronger as Malta's fighter defences chipped away, and on the last day of July a single reconnaissance SM79 appeared with nine Fiat CR42s in support. Three Gladiators, flown by Flt Lt Hartley, Fg Off Woods, and Fg Off Taylor, successfully drove the SM79 off but were set upon by the fighters. N5519, piloted by Hartley, was hit in the fuel tank. The aircraft burst into flames and crashed in the sea. Hartley baled out but was badly burned. HQ signalled the Air Ministry's casualty section, "Gladiator N5519 Luqa. In sea off Zonker Point Malta 31/7. Approx 1015 local time. 37364 F/Lt P.W. Hartley seriously injured, multiple burns of moderate severity". Emphasising the still-unofficial nature of the fighter flight, the casualty verification sheet notes: "Ledger gives 3 AACU Med HQ Malta" as his unit.

Hartley's fate hung in the balance as he lay in Imtarfa hospital, with "extensive burns legs, hands, forehead." It was not until two weeks after his crash that HQ Malta signalled that he appeared "to be out of immediate danger." The near-loss of Hartley, as one of the original four members of the flight, was a serious blow. The loss of N5519 was serious too. The Fighter Flight was now down to one Hurricane and two Gladiators serviceable.

By now the Air Ministry was alive to the need for proper fighter defences and took steps resulting in the formation of No.261 Squadron. On August 2, 12 Hurricanes of No.418 Flight were flown off HMS *Argus* and reached Malta a few hours later. As the new arrivals were prepared for operations, the Gladiators continued to hold the fort. Then, for a short time, a three-flight structure was set up allowing for the rotation of pilots, with six aircraft on stand-by every day, four Hurricanes and two Gladiators.

Ten days after No.418 Flight arrived, it was effectively combined with the Hal Far fighter flight – though the latter still had no official footing – to form No.261 Squadron, RAF. Sqn Ldr Martin stood down and the ad hoc arrangements made back in May finally came to an end.

In October 1940, the three remaining serviceable Gladiators were used more rather than less frequently. There were never enough Hurricanes to retire them completely, and in contrast to the fears expressed in June, they continued to prove useful. N5529 had its engine replaced with a unit from a written-off Blenheim, a Mercury XV fitted with a variable-pitch propeller and capable of using higher-octane fuel than the original powerplant. It proved successful so N5520 and N5531 were similarly modified.

The surviving Sea Gladiators continued to operate throughout the autumn and winter of 1940 and into the new year, first as part of No.261 Squadron and then reverting to the Fleet Air Arm when 806 Squadron arrived. The naval unit transferred ashore from HMS *Illustrious*, which had suffered severe damage at the hands of the Luftwaffe in January 1941. Its usual equipment was the Fairey Fulmar two-seat fighter, but it had operated a few Sea Gladiators too, and Fulmar losses meant the old Malta Gladiators were transferred to keep its numbers up. There were four in service at the end of January, possibly including N5513, which had been one of the aircraft taken from Kalafrana for HMS *Eagle* back in April 1940.

Numbers are slightly unclear thereafter. In the middle of February, part of 806 Squadron left for Crete, evidently taking at least one of its original Sea Gladiators, and the rest of the squadron embarked HMS *Formidable* in March. An account by Plt Off John Pain suggests when N5531 was wrecked in an air raid in February 1941, only N5520 remained, though a different story notes a Gladiator being destroyed in an air raid on Hal Far in March. In any event, only N5520 was complete by September 1941, having possibly remained with the FAA

BELOW: Lt Jackie Sewell brought down a Ju 88 on January 24, 1941, for the last Gladiator kill in Malta.
VIA CHRISTOPHER F SHORES

contingent at Hal Far. By then it had been unserviceable for some time. It was refurbished by No.185 Squadron and used for meteorological reconnaissance.

In February 1942, N5520 was wrecked, first by being turned over on landing by Sgt Jolly, then by damage from a bomb while it was in a dispersal pen. The engine and wings were removed for salvage and the stripped fuselage removed to a disused quarry, so as to be out of the way. There it remained until August 1943. Its significance recognised, the wrecked, incomplete aircraft was gifted to the people of Malta and has been on display since shortly afterwards.

Legacy

Malta's Sea Gladiators have a complex legacy. It is often considered today that their importance was overstated in early accounts – even when AVM Park presented N5520, he seemed aware of this and was careful not to challenge the legend of the famous biplanes. He fudged the nature of their contribution slightly, by rolling in their achievements with those of Hurricanes in the early months of the conflict. Nevertheless, it was a story that the RAF was happy to play on when Malta's safety was secured. The signals that betrayed the utter lack of confidence in them displayed by Air Cdre Maynard and Sir William Dobbie, and the truculent refusal of the Air Ministry to reinforce them, were kept safely out of public view until 1972. By this time, the 'great epic' of Malta was well and truly established. It is true that the Gladiators did not experience any significant success while they held the line alone, and only scored their initial victory after the first Hurricanes had arrived. Once the monoplanes were present, the Gladiators formed a diminishing part of the island's defence.

Yet the Gladiators did not fade away after Hurricanes arrived, and there were times in the early months when they held the line virtually alone again. They continued to engage and occasionally shoot down raiding Italian and German aircraft for the rest of 1940 and even into 1941. At least six were used, yet only one was shot down. The lack of extravagant success is unsurprising considering the pilots had no formal training in fighter operations, and they were learning as they went, along with the fighter control personnel they worked with. Given those circumstances, the concrete successes they did achieve were remarkable. And whether or not the successes were significant, the effect the small party of biplanes and their pilots and ground crew had on the morale of the island's population, military and civilian, was tangible and substantial. It is difficult to conclude that the legend of the Malta Gladiators is undeserved, even if it is much less simplistic than originally portrayed. ■

BELOW: The fuselage of N5520 in Valletta's Palace Square, on the occasion of its presentation to the people of Malta by the AOC Air Headquarters Malta, Air Marshal Sir Keith Park, on September 3, 1943.
IWM CM 5347

PEARL HARBOR

In terms of influencing the course of World War Two, few air actions can have had the dramatic effect of Japan's surprise attack on Pearl Harbor in December, 1941

WORDS: THOMAS McKELVEY CLEAVER

The Japanese attack on Pearl Harbor was, as Admiral Husband E Kimmel termed it, during his testimony to the investigating congressional committee: "A beautifully planned and executed military manoeuvre."

Years later, Richard H 'Dick' Best Jr, a member of VB-6 aboard USS *Enterprise* at the time, said: "The only thing really surprising about the attack to any of us in the navy at the time, was that it occurred the day it did, rather than any other day that year."

Pearl Harbor's vulnerability to surprise air attack was well known, having been demonstrated on February, 7, 1932, when then Captain, Ernest J King, brought USS *Saratoga* within striking range, without being spotted. This was during the Army/Navy Grand Joint Exercise 4 Blue, and he executed an air attack that umpires declared eliminated the base for further operations. To prove it wasn't a fluke, two further 'surprise attacks' occurred in 1935 and 1937 fleet exercises. When President Roosevelt ordered that Pearl Harbor would become the main Pacific Fleet base in May 1940, naval leaders warned it would put the fleet at risk of attack. Roosevelt hoped it would act as a deterrent, but the move put Pacific Fleet radio communications within range of the Japanese listening station on Kwajalein in the Marshall Islands. This was revealed in December 1940, when the Army Signal Corps tested a new speech-scrambler system for radio telephone calls to the US. When the scrambler was tested, an operator in Tokyo broke in to ask if there was a problem with the channel, since he could not understand the voice transmission.

Knowing the Japanese were monitoring calls was why General Marshall sent the final warning of the impending attack by commercial telegraph rather than by telephone. Best was wrong about the timing; it could only happen when it did, due to the constraints under which the Imperial Navy operated. The oil embargo which President Roosevelt had imposed following Japanese occupation of French Indochina in June 1941, meant Japan had to go to war no later than 1942 to take the Southeast Asian oilfields, while there was still oil and gasoline stockpiles to fight the necessary battles. Thus, planning was dominated by weather, specifically the northeast monsoon that spreads through Southeast Asia beginning in February. December and January were the two months with favourable weather for the Philippines, Malayan, and East Indies invasions; conditions for air operations would worsen until becoming impossible in May.

The two navies had viewed each other as potential adversaries since Admiral Togo's victory over the Russian Navy at the Battle of Tsushima Strait in 1905.

BELOW: Although this is a replica, the Nakajima B5N 'Kate' was a key component of the Japanese Navy's devastating attack.
PHILIP MAKANNA/GHOSTS

Decisive action

Japan's naval strategy came from Captain Alfred Mahan's *The Influence of Sea Power Upon History*, which had been translated into Japanese. His emphasis on a climactic battle confirmed their experience at Tsushima, so their World War Two plan involved seizing the Philippines and Guam, forcing the Americans to recover them. America's 'Orange Plans' began similarly, as both sides foresaw decisive fleet action north of the Marianas.

Given control of the Central Pacific after World War One, the Japanese changed to an 'attrition strategy', harrying the Americans from the new bases, so they arrived depleted, like the Russians had at Tsushima. In 1936, the Japanese cabinet adopted a plan to secure position in East Asia and extend influence to the South Seas. The Imperial Navy opposed a war involving the US and Britain. Isoroku Yamamoto, vice minister of the Japanese Navy, led the resistance, recalling his travels through the US in the 1920s: "Anyone who has seen the auto factories in Detroit and the oilfields in Texas, knows that Japan lacks the power for a war with America."

Following signing of the Tripartite Pact in November 1940, the situation was so threatening that special naval troops guarded the ministry, and Yamamoto changed residence nightly. Soon afterwards, the German raider *Atlantis* captured SS *Automedon* and top-secret documents were given to the Japanese – including British War Cabinet minutes of August 1940, admitting the indefensibility of Malaya and Hong Kong, and that Britain would not go to war over French Indochina. Knowing this, the navy accepted Foreign Minister Yōsuke Matsuoka's argument that the new alliance would deter the US and Britain. Admiral Yamamoto took command of the Combined Fleet.

On August 17, 1941, President Roosevelt warned Japan the US ▶

ABOVE:
The attack, taking place before the Japanese nation had declared war upon the United States came as a complete surprise.
US NATIONAL ARCHIVE

PEARL HARBOR

RIGHT: This photo, taken from a Japanese aircraft, shows ships moored on both sides of Ford Island shortly after the beginning of the December 7, 1941, attack. The view is approximately east, with the supply depot, submarine base and fuel farm in the right centre distance. A torpedo has just hit USS *West Virginia* on the far side of Ford Island (centre). Other battleships moored nearby are (from left): *Nevada, Arizona, Tennessee* (inboard of *West Virginia*), *Oklahoma* (torpedoed and listing) alongside *Maryland* and *California*. On the near side of Ford Island, to the left, are light cruisers *Detroit* and *Raleigh*, target and training ship *Utah* and seaplane tender *Tangier*. *Raleigh* and *Utah* have been torpedoed, and *Utah* is listing sharply to port. Japanese aircraft are visible in the right centre (over Ford Island) and over the Navy Yard at right. US Navy aircraft on the seaplane ramp are on fire. ORIGINAL IMPERIAL JAPANESE NAVY IMAGE VIA US NAVY ARCHIVES

would act if "neighbouring countries" were attacked. The main deterrent to an air attack on Pearl Harbor was the harbour's shallowness. The Type 91 aerial torpedo went so deep when dropped, it would mire in the bottom. However, the Royal Navy attack on the Italian fleet in the shallow Taranto harbour in November 1940, showed torpedoes could be modified. With that, attack planning proceeded, and Admiral Yamamoto proposed an attack on Pearl Harbor in January 1941; this overturned 20 years of naval plans, and the navy's general staff initially opposed him.

When Roosevelt's embargo left the country with barely enough resources to support two years of war, the general staff finally agreed to Yamamoto's plan.

By 1941, Japanese naval aviation was the equal of any and superior to most. Their six fleet carriers had experienced working together, unlike all other navies. The A6M2 fighter, D3A1 dive bomber, and B5N2 torpedo bomber were superior to all other naval aircraft.

The Type 91 aerial torpedo was the best in the world. War games in September 1941 revealed shortcomings that had to be fixed. Significantly, the exercise imposed radio silence; US naval intelligence continued to believe the fleet would remain in home waters. All that had to be done to ensure surprise was convince the Americans to continue that belief.

Formidable on paper

On November 5, 1941, an imperial conference concluded that if no diplomatic agreement could be reached with the US regarding the embargo by the beginning of

> **Pearl Harbor's vulnerability to surprise air attack was well known, having been demonstrated on February, 7, 1932, when then Captain, Ernest J King, brought USS Saratoga within striking range, without being spotted**

in Hong Kong had identified and tracked them. The navy held a week-long communications drill in mid-November that began when the carriers moved to their rendezvous in the Inland Sea. On November 17, the fleet's radio operators left the ships and continued these communications; this was by Morse Code, and an operator's 'fist' could be identified. Thus, the US radio monitors in Hawaii and the Philippines listened to familiar radiomen and checked the direction: the fleet was in Sasebo as expected. The carriers instituted strict radio silence when they left for the Kuriles on November 17. That day, Ambassador Joseph C Grew cabled that Japanese internal security was now so tight the embassy was no longer able to provide any early warning of warlike moves. A week later, a Gallup poll found 52% of Americans expected war with Japan. The six-carrier striking force departed Hokkaido on November 26. On December 1, fleet commander Admiral Chuichi Nagumo aboard his flagship *Akagi* received the message: "Climb Mount Niitaka." The attack was on. US naval cryptanalysts would not break the Imperial Navy's JN-25 code for another two months, so did not know that a daily radio broadcast from Tokyo contained updated information from a Japanese spy in Honolulu regarding Pacific Fleet ship movements, or the information that the US was not flying reconnaissance missions into the stormy northern Pacific. Japanese operational security had beaten American intelligence.

At dawn on December 7, the Japanese fleet arrived at their designated position northeast of Hawaii, out of range of US patrols. The first attack wave of 183 aircraft in three groups was launched, led by Commander Mitsuo Fuchida from *Akagi*. Four aircraft failed to get airborne because of technical difficulties and the 179 remaining headed west. The first group – whose targets were battleships and aircraft carriers – comprised 48 B5N2 bombers in four sections. They were armed with 1,760lb armour-piercing bombs, which were finned 16in battleship shells. A further 40 B5N2s, carried Type 91 torpedoes.

The second group – targeting the naval air station on Ford Island and the army's Wheeler Field – comprised 48 D3A1

RIGHT:
An Imperial Japanese Navy Mitsubishi A6M2 'Zero' on the aircraft carrier *Akagi* during the Pearl Harbor operation.
US NAVY

December, Japan would attack. Planners saw speed as essential to catch the enemy off guard. Allied forces appeared formidable on paper but were dispersed across the region rather than concentrated and suffered a lack of command unity, since three national armed forces faced a unified Japan. The war plan allowed 50 days to conquer the Philippines, 100 days for Malaya and 150 for the Indies.

When the carriers were sent south to support the move in Indochina, it was discovered the British radio monitoring station

PEARL HARBOR

ABOVE:
The Commemorative Air Force *Tora! Tora! Tora!* flight comprises replicas of key Japanese types involved in the Pearl Harbor attack such the A6M2 'Zero', Aichi D3A 'Val' and Nakajima B5N 'Kate'. PHIL MAKANNA/GHOSTS

dive bombers armed with 550lb general-purpose bombs. The 43 A6M2 fighters of the third group would attack aircraft at Ford Island, Hickam Field, Wheeler Field and the navy auxiliary fields at Barber's Point and Kaneohe.

Unknown to the Japanese, 500 miles south, USS *Enterprise*, delayed a day in returning to Pearl Harbor by the same bad weather, after ferrying 12 Marine F4F-3s of VMF-211 to Wake Island, turned into the wind 200 miles southwest of Pearl Harbor at 0615hrs to launch 18 SBD-2 and SBD-3 dive bombers. The Dauntlesses set off in nine formations of two, each pair assigned a segment of the search area between the ship and Hawaii. At the end of their patrols at 0730hrs, they were to head for NAS Ford Island. Because of radio silence, several back-seaters decided to practise radio homing, tuning their sets to Honolulu radio stations KGMB and KGU. At 0700hrs, Privates George Elliot and Joseph Lockard, at Ôpana Point on the northern end of Oahu, decided to keep their SCR-270 radar on and get some additional training, since the truck that was to take them to breakfast was late. The radar had arrived the previous August and had been installed a month earlier. At 0702hrs, Elliot saw a large blip on the screen, approaching from the north, 130 miles distant. Lockard telephoned the new information centre at Fort Shafter and reported they had spotted what Elliot described as "an awful big flight". The Fort Shafter operator passed the report to 2nd Lieutenant Kermit Tyler, who had arrived in Hawaii on December 1. Knowing a formation of B-17s was due from the mainland at any time, he told the privates not to worry. Their transportation arrived minutes later, so they shut down the radar.

Do not shoot!

At 0755hrs local time, Cdr Fuchida raised his binoculars as the formation came out of the mountainous valley north of Pearl Harbor and surveyed the target. There were no defending fighters airborne, no activity on any of the ships. Surprise had been achieved!

Fuchida ordered his radioman to send the code message for success: "Tora! Tora! Tora!"

At 0800hrs, VB-6 Senior Division Leader Lieutenant Dick Best

LEFT:
An astonishing moment in time. Two Imperial Japanese Navy Type 99 'Val' carrier-based bombers fly near a US Army Air Corps 38th Reconnaissance Squadron B-17E that arrived over Oahu from California in the middle of the Japanese air raid on Pearl Harbor. ARMY SIGNAL CORPS COLLECTION/US NATIONAL ARCHIVES

RIGHT:
The USS *Arizona* (BB-39) burning after the Japanese attack on Pearl Harbor, December 7, 1941. The ship is resting on the harbour bottom. The supporting structure of the forward tripod mast has collapsed after the forward magazine exploded.
US NATIONAL ARCHIVES

returned to his office next to the squadron ready room and flipped on the speaker that relayed the radio messages from the airborne aircraft. Three minutes later, all work was forgotten when he heard Ensign Manuel Gonzalez's high-pitched shout: "Don't shoot! This is an American plane! Do not shoot!" Gonzalez and wingman Ensign Fred Weber had just finished their search of the northernmost sector. As they turned away, they were suddenly surrounded by six unknown aircraft with fixed landing gear. Before Aviation Radioman 3/class Leonard Kozalek, could deploy his weapon, the Dauntless caught fire from the burst of fire by the strange aeroplanes. A second burst likely killed both he and Gonzales. As one Dauntless plummeted toward the ocean, carrying the first *Enterprise* fliers to die in the Pacific War, Ensign Weber dived and evaded his pursuers by weaving at 25ft above the waves. For the 36 *Enterprise* fliers, their invitation to World War Two read, 'come as you are'. Air group commander Cdr Howard 'Brigham' Young and Ensign Perry Teaff had just passed NAS Barber's Point when they spotted aircraft over the MCAS Ewa. Young observed it was early for the army to fly on a Sunday. Suddenly, anti-aircraft explosions blossomed over the field and Ensign Teaff spotted a low-wing single-engine aircraft closing on them. Bullet strikes stitched Young's tail and then Teaff saw the rising sun emblem, as the pilot turned for a second attack. Teaff's radioman unlimbered his single .30 machine gun as Young called: "Follow me!" and dived for the hills below.

Lieutenant Clarence E Dickinson was ready to bid farewell to his gunner, Aviation Radioman 3/ Class William C Miller, who would finish his navy enlistment on landing at Ford Island. Dickinson and wingman Ensign McCarthy were approaching Barber's Point at 1,500ft when he spotted explosions at Battleship Row. Climbing for a better look, the two were attacked by two strange fighters. The Americans dived away and ran into four more enemy fighters that quickly shot down McCarthy, who managed to bale out; he landed in a tree and broke his leg while his gunner, ARM3/c ▶

RIGHT:
A small boat rescues a seaman from the wrecked USS *West Virginia* which is burning in the foreground. Smoke rolling out amidships shows where the most extensive damage occurred. Note the two men in the superstructure. The USS *Tennessee* is seen inboard. This is a colourised version of an original black and white photograph.
US NATIONAL ARCHIVES

PEARL HARBOR

Mitchell Cohn, died in the crash. The other three pursued Dickinson. Bill Miller, wounded in the first pass, ran out of ammunition, and was hit by fire. One crossed Dickinson's nose and he fired his two guns, setting it on fire. Another fired, setting the left wing aflame. As the Dauntless spun in, Dickinson managed to get out at 1,000ft and throw himself off the wing. Miller was slumped over his gun. He landed in a sugarcane field in time to see the SBD explode. At Battleship Row, USS *West Virginia*, moored outboard of USS *Tennessee*, was hit by three of the 16in naval shell 'bombs' while two torpedoes exploded against her starboard side.

Petty Officer 1st Class Noburo Kanai peered through his bombsight as his B5N2 passed over the American battleships moored below. He tripped the release and the aircraft jumped as the near-ton of weight dropped free. He was able to watch the bomb as it arrowed down to disappear into the funnel of USS *Arizona*. As the B5N2 turned away, its bomb continued into the bowels of the battleship, penetrating the main magazine before finally exploding. Kanai reported that the force of the massive explosion nearly took down the bomber with him and his two crew mates in it.

Aces high

At Wheeler Field, second lieutenants Ken Taylor and George Welch of the 47th Pursuit Squadron were surprised by the sound of aircraft overhead and explosions on the airfield. Both had spent the night before in an all-night poker game that had only just wrapped up; they were still in the formal wear they had worn to the officer's club. Stepping outside, Taylor saw burning buildings and more explosions.

Taylor called Haleiwa field where the squadron had moved their aeroplanes and ordered P-40Bs be prepared for take-off. Welch started up his new Buick. He reached 100mph driving the 11 miles to Haleiwa, where they found their P-40s fuelled, but not fully armed. They attracted the attention of enemy fighters as soon as they were airborne. Evading them, they came on a bomber formation. Opening fire, Welch discovered his 50-cal nose guns were disconnected. Using the 30-cal wing guns, two of the enemy caught fire and fell away. Taylor's guns worked; he hit one and damaged another before both were both forced to break off with enemy fighters on their tails. The first wave disappeared as they landed at Wheeler. A senior officer ordered them to stay on the ground, but when the second wave appeared overhead, they set off into the swarming enemy. Welch managed to find another bomber formation and they attacked. Welch shot down two while Taylor downed a third, but then was hit by the rear gunner of number

ABOVE:
One of the seven Vought SB2U-3 Vindicators of US Marine squadron VMSB-231 destroyed on the field at Ewa during the December 7, 1941, attack on Pearl Harbor. All of VMSB-231's spares (the squadron was embarked in the USS *Lexington* (CV-2), en route to Midway, at the time) were thus destroyed. In the background is one of VMSB-232's Douglas SBDs. USMC

LEFT:
P-40s of the 47th Pursuit Squadron took off from Wheeler Field and saw action against the first and second waves of Japanese attacks.
PHILIP MAKANNA/GHOSTS

ABOVE:
Sheer devastation. Aircraft wreckage adjacent to a smashed hangar at the Ford Island Naval Air Station's seaplane base soon after the Japanese air raid.
US NATIONAL ARCHIVES

> **The oil embargo which President Roosevelt had imposed following Japanese occupation of French Indochina in June 1941, meant Japan had to go to war no later than 1942**

to Dorsett and said: "We're at war and I'll never get out of the navy alive." Dick Best remembered coming onto the flight deck moments later and looking up at the island. "The first thing I saw was the biggest American flag I had ever seen, flying from the masthead, and whipping in the wind. It was the most emotional sight of the war for me."

Enterprise's fighter commander, LCDR Clarence Wade McCluskey, rushed to the flag bridge to urge that the 18 F4F-3As of Fighting-6 be launched to help protect Pearl Harbor. Halsey demurred; with an enemy force of unknown size somewhere in the vicinity, the 18 fighters were needed to defend *Enterprise*. At 1645hrs, the admiral ordered a search-and-strike mission for the 18 TBD Devastators of Torpedo-6, with an escort of six Wildcats. In the event, the aircraft found nothing, as the Mobile Fleet had turned to the northwest after recovering its second Pearl Harbor strike. The torpedo bombers managed to recover without first dropping their torpedoes, but the effort took time, and the six fighters were ordered to fly on, in to Ford Island. It was a fatal order. Aboard *Akagi*, recently returned Commander Fuchida reported to Admiral Nagumo that the first wave had hit all their targets. He told the admiral there were no enemy ▶

four. Welch had just opened fire on number five when Welch radioed that he'd been wounded. Welch broke off to cover Taylor and they returned to Wheeler. Aboard *Enterprise*, Admiral William Halsey learned of the attack. Officer of the Deck Lieutenant John Dorsett ordered general quarters and the 19-year-old bugler Seaman Jim Barnill sounded the staccato notes of 'Boots and Saddles'. Boatswain's Mate 1/class Max Lee played his pipe over the 1MC then called: "General quarters! General quarters! All hands man your battle stations!" After the war, he remembered he then turned

LEFT:
Imperial Japanese Navy Type 99 Carrier Bomber, an Aichi D3A 'Val', shot down at Pearl Harbor during the December 7, 1941, attack.
US NATIONAL ARCHIVES

PEARL HARBOR

defences and that a third strike could destroy the fuel storage at Pearl Harbor, forcing the US Navy to abandon Hawaii. At that moment, a radio report from the second wave leader reported American fighters were attacking his formations. Nagumo shook his head. "We have done what we came to do."

At the same time, 'Fighting Six' commander LCDR Clarence Wade McCluskey led six Wildcats to escort the last 12 SBDs aboard in an unsuccessful search for the enemy. The little formation finally arrived over Pearl Harbor at night, lights out. When they spotted Ford Island, they switched on their lights. Shell shocked, trigger-happy gunners below saw the lights and immediately opened fire. Two Wildcats went down immediately, the survivors doused their lights and got away from the storm of fire. All were low on fuel and two pilots elected to bale out rather than try to land in the confusion below. McCluskey and Ensign Gale Herman managed to land; the gunners continued to fire at Herman as he taxied in from the runway. He found 18 bullet holes in the Wildcat and considered himself lucky. The two who had baled out spent a harrowing night in the cane fields trying to convince the defenders they were on the same side.

Hard hit

The Japanese had accomplished their goal. All the battleships were sunk or damaged. Ford Island and Wheeler Field had been hard hit. Losses were 188 aircraft destroyed and 159 damaged, for a total Japanese loss of 29. George Welch and Ken Taylor were the first to be awarded the Distinguished Service Cross. Welch was nominated for the Medal of Honor; it was denied when his superior officers claimed he had taken off without proper authorisation and against orders.

The makers of the 1970 movie, Tora! Tora! Tora! alleged that when he was informed of the success, Admiral Yamamoto said: "I fear all we have done is to awaken a sleeping giant and fill him with a terrible resolve." At least the sentiment was accurate. In the end, the Japanese mistake was to attack the US at all. Had Japan attacked the British and Dutch and ignored the US, Roosevelt may not have won support for the defence of distant Asian colonies. Had Congress not declared war to avenge Pearl Harbor, Hitler would not have kept his promises in the Tripartite Pact and declared war on the United States. Without the German declaration of war, the US would likely never have declared war unilaterally. While it would take two dangerous years for the full military force of the United States to be felt, Winston Churchill was right when he recorded that on the night of December 7, 1941, he "slept the sleep of the saved." Just before Christmas 1941, new naval aviator, Ensign John Bridgers, and 50 other naval aviators went aboard SS *President Hoover* with 2,000 construction workers, headed for Pearl Harbor. After a week at sea, Diamond Head came into view. Bridgers later recalled:

ABOVE:
An A6M2 'Zero' on display at the Pacific Air Museum, Pearl Harbor, is painted to represent BII-120 flown by Imperial Japanese Navy pilot Shigenori Nishikaichi. The original aircraft was shot down and destroyed but some fragments of the aircraft are also on display at the same location.
J J MESSERLEY CC BY-SA 3.0

LEFT:
Remember December 7th – a US government propaganda poster of 1942 sought to help galvanise Americans' determination to avenge a "Day of infamy."
US NATIONAL ARCHIVES

> **At dawn on December 7, the Japanese fleet arrived at their designated position northeast of Hawaii, out of range of US patrols**

LEFT: The wreckage of a Nakajima B5N-2 'Kate' from the Japanese aircraft carrier *Kaga*, being lifted by crane, at Pearl Harbor. The aircraft was shot down during the December 7 raid.
US NATIONAL ARCHIVES

"As we pulled into Pearl Harbor, I remembered having seen a newsreel with Secretary of the Navy Frank Knox maintaining that little substantial damage had been done to the Pacific Fleet by the Pearl Harbor attack. We saw that the waters were still oil covered, and we passed the grounded battleship USS *Nevada* in the channel. In the harbour were more derelicts… the capsized USS *Oklahoma*, the sunken USS *West Virginia,* and the remains of USS *Arizona*. It was evident there had been grievous hurt inflicted by the enemy." Like everyone who saw the results of the Pearl Harbor attack, Bridgers took an oath of vengeance. For the US Navy, the Pacific War was personal.

US AIRCRAFT OF WORLD WAR TWO

P-40Bs were among the first US aircraft to engage Imperial Japanese Navy aircraft during the surprise attack on the naval base at Pearl Harbor. This example '300' from the 78th Pursuit Group, was based at Bellows Field, one of the satellite airfields at Oahu. Fortunately, the site escaped the December 7 attack largely unscathed.
ALL PROFILES ANDY HAY-FLYINGART

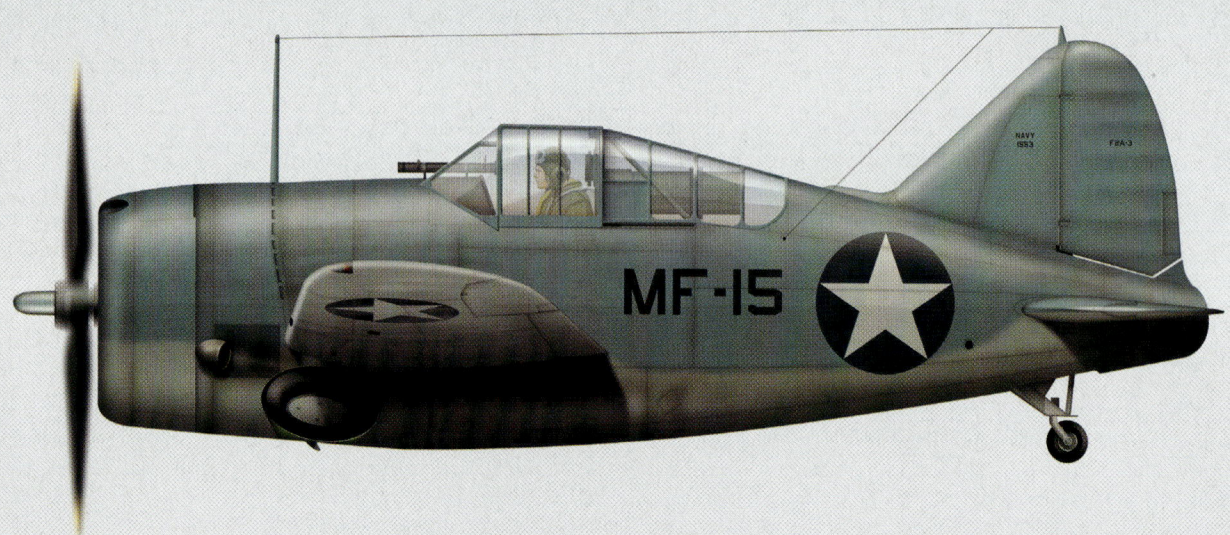

The US Marine's Brewster Buffalos were already obsolete compared to the Japanese A6M 'Zeros' they faced during the early stages of the June 1942 Battle of Midway. Nevertheless, Captain Bill Humberd was credited with shooting down an A6M Zero and a B5N 'Kate' torpedo bomber.

B-17F 230061 *Wolff Pack* was the usual mount of 2nd Lt Robert Wolff. The bomber suffered multiple bullet strikes while part of the lead formation to attack the Messerschmitt factories at Regensburg in August 1943. Wolff successfully brought the damaged B-17 back to its Norfolk base, only for it to be shot down the following month. 'Bob' Wolff was taken prisoner and survived the war.

The Consolidated B-24 Liberator was produced in higher numbers than any other bomber of World War two. This 'H' model, 42-52234 *Corky Burgendy Bombers* was delivered to the USAAF's 733rd Bomb Squadron of the 453rd Bomb Group at Old Buckenham, Norfolk, shortly before the launch of the Allies' so-called 'Big Week' offensive of February 1944.

Grumman F4F-4 Wildcat 'White 23' was flown by Lt Cdr John Thatch during the Battle of Midway. Leading the fighter squadron VF-3, Thatch as his fellow pilots flew escort duties in support of Devastator torpedo aircraft. The Wildcats encountered a group of 40 'Zeros' and Thatch was able to send one down in flames.

MIDWAY

MASSACRE OF MARINES AT MIDWAY

Within the US forces' crucial victory at the Battle of Midway was a punishing blow against the US Marine Corp's Brewster Buffalo squadrons

WORDS: ANDY THOMAS

ABOVE: The portly lines of the Brewster F2A-3 flown by VMF-221 are evident in this view of a wartime camouflaged aircraft.
US NAVY

Japan's unannounced strike against the United States at Pearl Harbor undoubtedly gave it a strategic advantage in the Pacific theatre, but just six months later momentum swung back in the Allies favour. The Imperial Japanese Navy's (IJN) plans to simultaneously destroy the US aircraft carrier fleet and the American military instillations at the mid-Pacific Midway atoll were intercepted by US intelligence.

Forewarned of Japan's intentions, US forces were able to effectively ambush the IJN forces and, during June 4-7, 1942, destroy four Japanese aircraft carriers and one heavy cruiser for the loss of one US carrier, the USS *Yorktown* and a destroyer. US Navy and Marine Corps airpower was the decisive element of the Battle of Midway but alongside their undoubted triumph was a painful lesson about the obsolescence of

one of its front-line fighters, the Brewster Buffalo.

The type, which was to gain an unenviable record for mediocrity, had its origins in a 1935 requirement for a new generation of fighters for the United States Navy. The US Navy's first Brewster F2A squadron was VF-2 under Lt Cdr Warren Harvey aboard the USS *Saratoga* that introduced them into service on December 8, 1939. The next F2A squadron was VF-2 that was largely manned by non-commissioned pilots and that took its Brewsters aboard the USS *Lexington* in March 1941 for a training cruise to Hawaii. However, within weeks of the outbreak of the war against Japan both units were re-equipped with the robust F4F Wildcat and their F2As were passed onto the US Marine Corps. Following the attack on Pearl Harbor, VMF-221 (that had been formed at San Diego on July 11, 1941) was embarked in the *Saratoga* for the relief of Wake Island. However, with the island's capture the squadron was diverted north to Midway Island where its 14 F2As arrived on Christmas Day. Under Maj V J McCaul, VMF-221 became part of Marine Air Group 22 on March 1, the same day VMF-212 was formed under Maj Harold W Bauer at MCAS Ewa on Hawaii, also with F2As.

Opening shots

The combat debut for the USMC Brewsters came soon afterwards on March 10 when a pair of Kawanishi H8K4 'Mavis' flying boats left Wotje Atoll in the Marshall Islands and one of them headed for Midway. This aircraft was detected by radar some 45 miles west of Midway and a dozen of VMF-221's F2As led by Captain Robert M Haynes were vectored out to intercept the intruder. One section of four led by Capt James L Neefus who was flying 01537/221-MF-1 caught the Mavis at 10,000ft and after making several firing passes the four-engine flying boat was shot down. However, as Brewster F2A 01524/221-MF-9 flown by Marine Gunner Dickey made a tail approach it was hit by fire from the flying boat's gunners and Dickey was wounded in the shoulder. James Neefus was credited with the first F-2A victory in US service. Apart from being the first enemy aircraft shot down by VMF-221, the action was significant. This Japanese flying boat had been assigned to carry out a photographic reconnaissance of Midway to provide intelligence for the major Japanese assault on the atoll planned for early June and could thus be regarded as the opening shot of the battle.

Towards the end of the month VMF-221 received a reinforcement of eight more aircraft and some additional pilots and at the end of May the squadron was further augmented. Thus, at the end of the month VMF-221, now commanded by Maj Floyd 'Red' Parks had 21 F2A-3s and seven F4F-3 Wildcats, the latter having been delivered a few days earlier by the USS *Kitty Hawk*. The Marines in VMF-221 learned that they were likely the intended target of a major Japanese amphibious operation when the commander in chief of the Pacific Fleet, Admiral Chester W Nimitz, paid them a personal visit on May 2.

Scramble!

The major operation by the Imperial Japanese Navy against ▶

> **❝ Alongside their undoubted triumph was a painful lesson about the obsolescence of one of its front-line fighters, the Brewster Buffalo ❞**

LEFT: F2A-3 2-MF-13 of VMF-212 sits in a camouflaged revetment at Ewa Field, Hawaii on April 25, 1942, soon after the unit had formed. US NAVY

BELOW: This VMF-221 F2A-3 is believed to be 'MF-17' seen before the red in the US markings was deleted. It was flown on June 4 by 2/Lt Charles Kunz when he shot down two D3A 'Val' dive bombers. P MERSKY

MIDWAY

ABOVE: A newly camouflaged Brewster F2A-3 wearing the markings carried at the Battle of Midway. US NAVY

Midway began early on June 4 when Admiral Nagumo's four fleet carriers *Akagi, Hiryū, Kaga,* and *Sōryū* with the light carriers *Zuihō* and *Hōshō* launched over one hundred aircraft against the island.

On Midway shortly before 0600hrs the strike was detected some 90 miles to the northwest and the air raid alarm was sounded shortly after some B-17s had got airborne to attack the Japanese ships. Having been on alert at 0600hrs, the fighters of VMF-221 led by Maj 'Red' Parks began to get airborne. 2/Lt John Musselman who was duty officer and recalled: "At 0559 the air raid siren sounded, and all the 'planes immediately took off. At 0615 Captain McCarthy and Second Lieutenant Corry landed to re-gas, having been on patrol since 0400. I immediately notified the command post and at the same time noticed enemy bombers approaching Sand Island. At 0630 enemy bombers hit Eastern Island, I just made the nearest slit trench. The bombing attack lasted for approximately two minutes. The nearest bombs landed about 100 yards from the ready tent causing no damage. During the strafing attack that followed, Second Lieutenant Phillips and I were in the dug-out. Approximately at 0700 the attack was over."

The squadron had launched in five divisions with Maj Parks leading the first two of 11 Buffalos, as 2/Lt Hughes had returned with engine troubles. About 15 minutes later when at 14,000ft and 30 miles from Midway, Parks spotted a big formation of D3A 'Val' dive bombers with their Zero escort. He immediately ordered his divisions to engage them but in their obsolescent Brewsters the inexperienced Marines in the CO

RIGHT: The surviving pilots from the Battle of Midway at Ewa Field, Hawaii on June 22, 1942. All but one are members of VMF 221. L-R: Capt Marion E Carl; Capt Kirk Armistead; Maj Raymond Scollin (MAG 22); Capt Herbert T. Merrill; 2/Lt Charles M Kunz; 2/Lt Charles S Hughes; 2/Lt Hyde Phillips; Capt Philip R White, and 2/Lt Roy A Corry, Jr. US NAVY

LEFT:
A USMC Brewster F2A 3 refuelling in a camouflaged dispersal on May 1, 1942. US NAVY

division were overwhelmed. Only two pilots survived, both from Capt Daniel Hennessey's second division, one of whom was Capt Phillip White who made the only claims from this overwhelmed formation. He wrote: "Captain Hennessy led us in an attack on the horizontal bombers. There were three formations of nine 'planes to the formation. After the first pass I lost my wingman and rest of the division. I made a long low fast climb and made a second above side pass, and started for a third, when I saw a 'Zero' fighter climbing up on my tail very rapidly. I pushed my stick forward as hard as I could and went into a violent dive. When I recovered and looked around, I had lost the Zero." Having lost the rest of the formation, White then spotted a straggler: "I made a long fast above side pass on this 'plane which I had spotted. After the pass I saw him waver and make an easy left turn into the water. He was at approximately 1,000ft when I initiated the pass. I believe I shot the pilot. The plane was [an] Aichi 99 dive-bomber. I again regained my altitude and saw another Aichi 99 weaving in and out of the clouds, returning to his carrier. I gave my Buffalo all the power I could get, and I finally gained enough to make a pass. I believe that I had damaged his engine and found out that I was out of ammunition. I am sure that I shot the rear seat gunner in this 'plane. I returned to the base and rearmed and took off and later received instructions to land." His was the only aircraft of the first two divisions to return.

Wildcats engaged

Leading VMF-221's second element, Capt Kirk Armistead had followed with his eight Buffalos and a Wildcat whilst the six F4F-3s ▶

BELOW:
Brewster F2A-3 01522 '221-MF-6' VMF 221 seen in the spring of 1942 was flown on June 4 by 2/Lt Charles Hughes but returned to Midway early with a malfunctioning engine. VIA P MERSKY

MIDWAY

ABOVE: Seen in the sand on Midway after the action on June 4, F4F-3 Wildcat 4008 '22' of VMF-221 was flown by Capt John F Carey who was wounded but had claimed an Aichi D3A 'Val' destroyed.
US NAVY

of the fifth division were led by Capt John Carey. The Buffalos and Wildcats climbed for height with Armistead's group arriving after a few minutes where the two divisions soon split into smaller elements. They fared little better, though the F4F pilots claimed six destroyed while the F2A pilots claimed four destroyed with several more damaged.

At 0616hrs CPO Juzo Mori, flying a Val from *Sōryū,* saw the coast of Midway dead ahead but within seconds, the two Vals in front of him exploded, almost certainly the victims of F4F-3s flown by Capt John Carey and 2/Lt Clayton Canfield. The latter, who was Capt Carl's wingman recorded: "We went out there and contacted them and there were about 19 carrier dive-bombers escorted by approximately ten 'Zero' fighters. The dive-bombers were in four and five plan 'Vs and the fighters were about 2,000ft above them. There were only three of us. At 0612, Captain Carey made a wide diving turn while reporting 'Tally Ho, large formation of bombers,' a slight pause, then, 'Accompanied by fighters.' The bombers were at approximately 12,000ft. I slid into a column on Captain Carey. I fired at the number three 'plane in the number three section until it exploded and went down in flames. I momentarily lagged looking for 'planes following us and went around the cloud the opposite direction from Captain Carey to have a better look behind, we were attacked by their fighters. I saw a large trail of smoke and the bomber burning on the ocean, but no fighters, and then joined up on him again. He headed in the general direction of the islands on an unsteady course. Finally, I observed that he was badly wounded, and he turned the lead over to me." The pair landed their damaged Wildcats with the airfield under attack by strafing fighters. Canfield concluded: "When the 'plane had stopped sliding, I jumped out and ran for a trench, while a 'plane was strafing in the direction of my abandoned 'plane." The third member of this section was Capt Marion Carl who wrote afterwards: "I made a high side on one of the fighters which was some 2,000' below me. My fire passed through my target, and I pulled away and up." He later described the next few minutes in an interview: "The next thing I knew, I had a Zero on my tail. I didn't know he was there until these tracers started going by. I racked it into a tightest turn I could. He followed me and made it look easy! So, I headed for the nearest cloud. He hit me eight times." Carl then set course for base

RIGHT:
2/Lt Charles Kunz shot down two dive bombers off Midway on June 4 but was wounded by the escorting Zeros.
MRS GRACE KUNZ VIA P MERSKY

RIGHT:
Maj Floyd Parkes the commander of VMF-221 who died leading his squadron at Midway. US NAVY

VMF-221, JUNE 4, 1942 BATTLE OF MIDWAY

Plane No.	Bu.No.	Pilot	Status
FIRST DIVISION (F2A-3)			
MF-1	01518	Maj Floyd B Parks	MIA
MF-2	01548	2Lt Eugene P Madole	MIA
MF-3	01525	Capt John R Alvord	MIA
MF-4	01537	2Lt John M Butler	MIA
MF-5	01569	2Lt David W Pinkerton Jr	MIA
MF-6	01552	2Lt Charles S Hughes	RTB early
SECOND DIVISION (F2A-3)			
MF-7	01552	Capt Daniel J Hennessey	MIA
MF-8	01541	2Lt Ellwood Q Lindsay	MIA
MF-9	01524	Capt Herbert T Merrill	Baled out WIA
MF-10	01528	2Lt Thomas W Benson	MIA
MF-11	01568	Capt Phillip R White	Survived
MF-12	01542	2Lt John D Lucas	MIA
THIRD DIVISION (F2A-3)			
MF-13	01562	Capt Kirk Armistead	Survived
MF-14	01563	2Lt William B Sandoval	MIA
MF-15	01553	Capt William C Humberd	Survived
MF-16	01523	2Lt Williams V Brooks	WIA
MF-17	01521	2Lt Charles M Kunz	WIA
MF-18	01559	2Lt Martin E Mahannah	KIA
23 (F4F-3)	3989	2Lt Walter W Swansberger	MIA
FOURTH DIVISION (F2A-3)			
MF-19	01520	Capt Robert E Curtin	MIA
MF-20	01550	2Lt Darrell D Irwin	Survived
FIFTH DIVISION (F4F-3)			
22	4008	Capt John F Carey	WIA
24	4000	Capt Marion E Carl	Survived
25	3997	2Lt Clayton M Canfield	Survived
26	4006	Capt Francis P McCarthy	MIA
27	2532	2Lt Roy A Corry	Survived
28	1864	2Lt Hyde Phillips	RTB early

and eventually descended. He was within two miles of the airfield when he encountered more Japanese fighters as he continued in his report: "I saw three Zero fighters at a low altitude that were making a wide circle, so I came down in a dive with almost full throttle. I gave him a long burst, until he fell off on one wing and when last seen was out of control headed almost straight down with smoke streaming from the 'plane. The other two fighters had cut across and were closing on me, so I headed for a cloud. I felt the impact of bullets striking the throttle, throw the 'plane into a skid, and he overran me. I raked him with gun fire as he went by. He slid across in front and below me, and I shoved over sharply and pressed the trigger at the same time. A few minutes later at 0720 received an order to land. In my opinion, I shot down one Zero fighter and inflicted unknown damage to two more."

Battling Buffalos

At the controls of F2A-3 Buffalo 01562/MF-13 Capt Kirk Armistead had led off the second of VMF-221's formations from Midway at 0602hrs, the Buffalos comprising four sections of two and a single Wildcat flown by 2/Lt Walter Swansberger. Armistead reported: "I climbed ▶

RIGHT:
The aircraft carrier *Akagi* and (left to right) *Sōryū*, *Hiryū*, and three battleships seen before the battle. US NAVY

MIDWAY

RIGHT: The pilots of VMF-221 at Ewa Hawaii on July 14 – many are survivors of Midway. Rear L-R: Unknown; 2/Lt Darrell D Irwin; 2/Lt Hyde Phillips; 2/Lt Roy A Corry Jr; 2/Lt Charles M Kunz. Seated L-R: 2/Lt William V Brooks; 2/Lt John C Musselman Jr; Capt Phillip R White; Capt William C Humberd; Capt Kirk Armisted; Capt Herbert T Merrill; Capt Marion E Carl; 2/Lt Clayton M Canfield. US NAVY

BELOW: Flying an F4F-3 Capt Marion Carl engaged the fighter escort, and his fire struck several Zeros. US NAVY

the division to 12,000ft and vector 310. At about 0620 I heard Capt Carey transmit 'Tally-Ho' then started climbing, and sighted the enemy at approximately 14,000ft at a distance of five to seven miles out, and approximately two miles to my right. I immediately turned, endeavouring to get a position above and ahead of the enemy and come down out of the sun. However, I was unable to reach this point in time. I was at 17,000ft when I started my attack. The target consisted of five divisions of from five to nine 'planes each, flying in division Vees. I figured this group to consist of from 30 to 40 dive-bombers of the Aichi type 99 SE DB. I was followed in column by five F2A-3 fighters and one F4F-3. I made a head on approach from above at a steep angle and at very high speed on the fourth enemy division which consisted of five 'planes. I saw my incendiary bullets travel from a point in front of the leader, up thru his 'plane and back through the 'planes on the left wing of the Vee. I continued in my dive, and looking back, saw two or three of those 'planes falling in flames." He was credited with probably destroying a Val and the aircraft he reported falling were probably those attacked by others of his formation, but when the Zero escort intervened, four Buffalos also went down.

Leading the second pair in Armistead's division was Capt Bill Humberd who was credited with an A6M Zero and a B5N 'Kate' torpedo-bomber. He wrote: "Our division of six 'planes, Capt Kirk Armistead is division leader. Sight contact was made of enemy formations at approximately 12,000ft bearing about 30° to port and distance of about 10-15 miles. We continued climbing to 17,000ft, still keeping the enemy slightly to our port, then when in position of about 3,500 to 4,000ft above and still to port we made attack, about 30-35 miles bearing 320° from islands. I followed division leader in a high side approach shooting down one bomber in this approach, then coming up for high side approach on other side I again attacked, thinking I might have shot down another bomber in this approach. I came up on other side and started another approach when, about half-way through run, I heard a loud noise and turning around I saw a large hole in hood of my plane and also two Zero navy fighters on me about 200 yards astern. I immediately pushed over in steep dive in which one followed me. I descended to water level in trying to gain distance on the fighter, the 'plane staying with me; I stayed at water level with full throttle gaining distance slowly until I decided the distance was great enough to turn

ABOVE:
An F4F-3 Wildcat taxies across the dust of Midway's airstrip. US NAVY

on 300yd distant, fired and the 'plane caught on fire and out of control dived in the water."

The recently arrived 2/Lt Charles Kunz was flying F2A-3 1521/MF-17, and he too recalled the action: "Our division was in the air at 0602 when the radar vectored us out on a heading of 320°. We had been climbing at almost full throttle and sighted about 40 enemy 'planes in five to nine 'plane divisions. Shortly after reaching 17,000ft, I saw Capt Armistead make his attack and Capt Humberd, my attack was a high speed, overhead approach. I was firing at the fifth last division and saw two 'planes in flames in the fourth division, very likely shot by Armistead and Humberd. It is my belief that Lt Sandoval was drawn flat in his approach and was shot by an enemy back seat gunner. I saw my target burst into flames and pull out of formation.

"After the initial attack, our division was completely separated, and I zoomed up on the starboard side of the enemy Aichi type 99 SE DB formation. I was about 2,000ft above the formation when I made my second attack. I used the above side approach and was firing short bursts frequently when this target caught fire. The pilot on the port outboard side of the Vee pulled out of formation to apparently let the 'plane on fire next to him get out. I started firing short burst at long range at the 'plane that left the formation when I was attacked. I was at an altitude of about 9,000ft, and shoved over in a dive trying to shake the 'plane on my tail until I was about 20ft from the water. I was making radical turns hoping the pilot couldn't get steadied on me. I glanced out of the rear and saw that it was a type Zero Sen navy fighter. I continued flying on a rapid turning course at full throttle when I was hit in the head by a glancing bullet. After he fired a few short bursts he left as I had been in a general direction of 205° heading away from the island. My 'plane was badly shot up and I knew it could not be used in another attack due to radio being shot and hydraulic system out. I flew for 10 or 15 minutes on this heading and circled until 0730 at which time I came in to the island and made my proper identifying approach and landed. I landed at 0750. I was very dizzy due to wound in head, immediately went to dispensary. I expended 312 rounds from three of my guns. In my opinion the Zero fighter has been far underestimated. I think it is probably one of the finest fighters in the present war." Charles Kunz recorded in his flying logbook: *F2A-3 01521. Combat with enemy (2 bombers) AICHI Type 99.*

This was Kunz's final flight in a Buffalo and the last occasion that the F2A saw combat in American hands. On June 6, the squadron could field just a trio each of F2A-3s and F-4F-3s.

Of the sacrifice of VMF-221, Capt Phillip White said: "It is my belief that any commander that orders pilots out for combat in an F2A-3 should consider the pilot as lost before leaving the ground." Kunz held a similar view later telling his wife: "The 'plane should have been relegated to training duties, which, of course, it was immediately after Midway."

For its gallant actions during the Battle of Midway, VMF-221 was awarded a Presidential Unit Citation, but this came at a huge sacrifice. A total of 15 F2A-3s and two F4F-3s were lost along with 14 pilots; four others were wounded. Nonetheless, actions later in the day turned Midway into a decisive victory for the Americans that turned the tide of the war in the Pacific. ■

> **As Brewster F2A 01524/221-MF-9 flown by Marine Gunner Dickey made a tail approach it was hit by fire from the flying boat's gunners and Dickey was wounded in the shoulder**

JAPANESE AIRCRAFT OF WORLD WAR TWO

Lieutenant Commander Shigeru Itaya led the first wave of the Pearl Harbor attack from the Imperial Japanese Navy aircraft carrier *Akagi* in Mitsubishi A6M2 'Zero' AI-155. He also saw combat during the Battle of Midway, but ultimately lost his life in a 'friendly fire' incident in 1944. ALL PROFILES ANDY HAY-FLYINGART

BI-151 of the Imperial Japanese Navy's 2nd Carrier Division, *Soryu*, during the Battle of Midway. The A6M2 type 'Zero' was more than a match for the early US fighters but the failure to develop more powerful engines eventually made it less competitive against later Allied types.

A6M2 'Zero' BII-144, was part of the *Hiryu* Air Group, 4th FCU during the attack on Pearl Harbor. It survived its participation in the second wave attack.

Mitsubishi A6M2 'Zero' EII-102 from the carrier *Zuikaku*'s fighter squadron was flown by Petty Officer 1st Class Tetsuzō Iwamoto on combat air patrols during the Pearl Harbor attack. Iwamoto did not see combat that day, but he went on to become one of Japan's highest scoring 'Aces' of the war with as many as 87 'kills' to his name.

BII-124 of the 2nd Carrier Division, *Hiryu*. Despite the 'Zero's' many successful combats against US Navy and Marine aircraft during the Battle of Midway, it could not prevent a crushing defeat of the Japanese forces in the Pacific theatre.

OPERATION JUBILEE

DOGFIGHTS OVER DIEPPE

Operation Jubilee, the Dieppe raid, was a costly defeat for the Allies that went on to pay dividends on D-Day. It was perhaps the largest single day air battle of the war.   **WORDS:** ANDY THOMAS

By the summer of 1942 the Spitfire was by some measure the most important fighter flown by the RAF operating across the Channel on fighter sweeps. Most units still flew the Spitfire Vb which was outclassed by the Focke Wulf FW 190s employed in increasing numbers by the *Luftwaffe* in JG 2 and JG 26 - the main units defending northern France. As an interim solution the Spitfire IX had quickly been developed and these were now proving the equal of the FW 190 that had been given the epithet of 'Butcher Bird' by the hard-pressed RAF fighter pilots.

The Spitfire IX was a marriage of the powerful Merlin 61 (and later Merlin 63) engine with the Mk V airframe that retained the older Mark's superb handling with a greatly improved overall performance.

Although introduced as a stopgap, the Spitfire IX became Fighter Command's standard aircraft for the rest of the war. They first entered service with 64 Squadron at Hornchurch under Sqn Ldr Wilf Duncan-Smith and were declared operational at the end of July. Within days the Canadian 401 Squadron was re-equipped with the Spitfire IX and began ops from Biggin Hill on August 3 while two days later 611 Squadron flew its first Mk IX operation. Then, on August 13 the Canadian 402 Squadron from Kenley began Mk IX operations, escorting USAAF B-17s of the 97th Bomb Gp in a raid on rail yards at Rouen. Squadrons had been placed on readiness for an attack on the port of Dieppe code-named Operation Rutter, but this had been cancelled. However, the raid on Dieppe, now code-named Operation Jubilee was planned for August 19 that was to result in perhaps the greatest air battle over western Europe of the war.

Duels over Dieppe

For the raid, fighter squadrons of Fighter Command's 10, 11, and 12 Groups were concentrated on airfields along the south coast to ensure complete cover over Dieppe and the assault shipping during daylight hours. As well as the four squadrons now flying the new Spitfire Mk.IX and the two with the specialised high-altitude Mk.VI, the force included no fewer than 42 squadrons flying the Spitfire Mk.V.

Well before dawn as the landing force edged towards the coast the first elements of the top cover prepared to take-off. At West Malling for example 610 Squadron was at readiness by 0300hrs. First off at 0415hrs, however, was 111 Squadron from Kenley led by Sqn Ldr Peter Wickham flying Spitfire Vb EP166/JU-N followed five minutes later by Sqn Ldr Desmond McMullen's 65 Squadron from Eastchurch; their task was to cover the Blenheims of 13 and 614 Squadrons laying a smoke screen to blind enemy coastal batteries. They arrived over Dieppe at 0440hrs with 111

BELOW: For the original attack on Dieppe named Operation Rutter, participating aircraft received identification stripes as displayed on Spitfire Vb BM579/FN-B of 331 Squadron Flown by Lt Rolf Berg. He shot down an FW 190 and damaged two more over Dieppe before being hit and forced to bale out.
VIA TOR LARSEN

Squadron's pilots noting that the stars were still shining. They were the first of a stream of fighters that covered the area throughout the day. Sqn Ldr Wickham for example flew five sorties during the operation – two leading his own 111 Squadron and three at the head of the inexperienced US 308th Fighter Squadron equipped with Spitfire Vbs and during the course of which he damaged two FW 190s. Other Spitfires were tasked with attacking gun emplacements and on one such sortie Fg Off Harry Jones' aircraft from 129 Squadron became the first to be lost. Then on his way back Jones' wingman, Sgt Reeves, had the Spitfire's first, albeit inconclusive brush with the Luftwaffe. As 65 and 111 Sqns departed, 124 Squadron's high altitude Spitfire VIs in company with the American-manned 71 (Eagle) Squadron led by Wg Cdr Myles Duke-Wooley were over the ships, being joined by Wg Cdr 'Dutch' Hugo's Hornchurch Wing (81, 122, 154, and 340 Squadrons). As the scale of the assault became evident, the Luftwaffe began appearing, but this initial group had only inconclusive brushes. Four Polish squadrons relieved them and they in turn were replaced by 402, 602, and 611 Squadrons as the sun rose above the horizon; and again, there were several skirmishes.

And so, the long day started. The Tangmere Wing arrived over the port soon after 0600hrs to cover a Boston attack whilst also up was Sqn Ldr Douglas Watkins'

> **The Spitfire IX had quickly been developed and these were now proving the equal of the FW 190**

611 Squadron. He recalled: "At 06.10 a FW190 dived down to my height (1,500ft) and swept round behind my No 2. I throttled back and easily turned inside the e/a [enemy aircraft] and fired a short burst at 45° deflection - I saw one cannon strike behind the e/a cockpit, and he flew straight inland over the River Bethune at 100ft. The e/a apparently tried to make a forced landing on the high ground SW of the river mouth and hit the ground bouncing into the air in a cloud of dust." The first victory of the day also made him an 'ace'.

By the time Wg Cdr David Scott-Malden's North Weald Wing comprising 242 Squadron led by Sqn Ldr Tom Parker with the Norwegians of 331 and 332 Squadrons as top cover appeared over the ships shortly before 0700hrs, the Luftwaffe's reaction began in earnest. No 332 Squadron soon became embroiled in a terrific dogfight losing two Spitfires but shooting down three Focke Wulfs. Sgt Marius Eriksen got one of them: "Just off coast, we were attacked by FW 190s. I managed to get on the tail of one of the four FW 190s which were trying to get into position for attack on one of our Spitfires. I gave him a burst and observed hits. The FW 190 turned on his back, but the

ABOVE:
The RAF's answer to the Focke Wulf was the Spitfire IX and the first were delivered to 64 Squadron in July 1942 and saw considerable action over Dieppe.
P H T GREEN COLLECTION

BELOW:
Sqn Ldr Peter Wickham of 111 Squadron stands in front of Spitfire Vb EP166/JU-N in which he flew five sorties over Dieppe on August 19. On the fateful day he damaged two Messerschmitt Bf 109s. The Spitfire carries 111's pre-war black bar marking on the nose. 111 SQN RECORDS

OPERATION JUBILEE

> **"The raid on Dieppe, now code-named Operation Jubilee was planned for August 19"**

enemy aircraft turned back into level position giving me opportunity to close in on him from rear. I gave him 2-3 bursts observing hits all the time. The E/A again turned on his back and dived down with smoke pouring out of the engine. He did not pull out of this dive, and he hit the sea with a huge splash." However, his CO, Maj Wilhelm Mohr who post war became head of the Royal Norwegian Air Force, was wounded by an FW 190 whilst Sgt Per Bergsland was shot down; he later took part in the 'Great Escape' and made it to freedom. Also successful was 331 Squadron whose CO, Maj Helge Mehr claimed the second of his six victories: "I remember that first clash with the Luftwaffe in the morning. During the dog-fight my No 2 was hit by a FW 190 and had to bale out. I managed to turn in behind the 190s and closed on the rear one. I put a good 4-5 second burst into him. He emitted black smoke, the pilot jumped out of his aircraft, which then turned over into a vertical dive." Another Norwegian who became an outstanding leader, Capt Kai Birksted claimed his second victory in this action. With 12½ confirmed between them the two Norwegian squadrons were the most successful of the day.

Another European exile unit in action was the Belgian-manned 350 Squadron. On this first mission Flt Lt Yvan du Monceau de Bergendael was flying EN794/MN-X and shot down an FW 190 as he noted in his flying log book: 'Attack with Blue section some FW 190s. One goes down spinning and in flames off Dieppe after one second burst.' Other pilots shared a second FW 190. Fighter cover continued from the West Malling Wing in which 610 Squadron was led by Sqn Ldr Johnnie Johnson and were attacked by 50 enemy fighters. Johnson shot an FW 190 into the sea before sharing a Bf 109 to claim his first victories of the year. In the intense fight Flt Lt Denis Crowley-Milling flying EP361/DW-H attacked a Messerschmitt Bf 109 off the tail of a Spitfire. His first burst found its mark, flipping the Messerschmitt over streaming glycol before the pilot baled out.

USAAF involvement

The first taste of real action for the new Spitfire-equipped USAAF fighter groups came during the Dieppe raid when the 31st FG saw action. In company with the RAF's 130 and 131 Squadrons, a dozen Spitfires of the 309th Fighter Squadron (FS) left Westhampnett early for Dieppe. Over the beachhead they were attacked by a swarm of FW 190s and in the ensuing dogfight Lt Samuel F Junkin Jr managed to shoot one down to claim the first fighter victory for the USAAF in Europe. However, moments later he was attacked and wounded himself by a second Focke-Wulf, he managed to bale out but was rescued by a torpedo boat that also picked up Lt Collins.

Also over Dieppe in a 308th FS Spitfire was Capt Frank Hill, who, having left Kenley at around 0700hrs recalled: "We arrived over the target area on time and split into four-ship formations. Patrolling the area, we were about 8,000 to 10,000ft. About that time, 12-plus enemy aircraft were reported by ground control and they arrived shortly thereafter at about 12,000ft. They immediately pressed home the attack, and a general dogfight resulted, with the Spitfires staying in sections of four, and the Focke-Wulfs and 109s mostly staying in

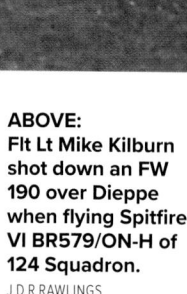

ABOVE: Flt Lt Mike Kilburn shot down an FW 190 over Dieppe when flying Spitfire VI BR579/ON-H of 124 Squadron.
J D R RAWLINGS

LEFT: When flown over Dieppe on August 19, Spitfire Vb EP130/NK-Y of 118 Sqn flown by Sgt Tommy de Courcey shared in shooting down a Dornier 217 with Wg Cdr Pat Gibbs.
C ANDERTON

pairs. After about 3 minutes of trying to keep my section from being hit, I finally caught a FW-l90 and fired about a 4-second burst of cannon and machine gun shells into it at about 300 yards, at about a 45-degree angle on his port side. He rolled and spun down with the smoke coming out, and as I last saw him, he was about 2,000ft still in a steep dive. The action was much too hot to take time to follow him all the way down." Credited with a probable, this was his first claim.

It had, however, been a difficult blooding as the inexperienced group lost eight Spitfires with others damaged resulting in one pilot dead, one missing and three as prisoners. During 123 sorties that day, two future aces, Maj Harrison Thyng, CO of the 309th and Lt John H White of the 307th also claimed probables.

Thirty miles from Dieppe was the major fighter base at Abbeville against which an attack by two-dozen B-17s of the 97th Bomb Group was planned for mid-morning. The four squadrons of Spitfire IXs escorted them and as bombs rained onto the airfield a dozen or so fighters were seen to take-off, and these attacked as the force departed. One of those engaged was Plt Off Don Morrison of 401 Squadron, as he recalled later for the RCAF Official History: "I saw a single FW 190 just ahead and about 1,500ft below me. I did a slipping barrel roll, losing height and levelled out about 150yds behind and slightly to the starboard and above the enemy aircraft. I opened fire with a 2-second burst closing to 25 yards. I saw strikes all along the starboard side of the fuselage and several pieces which seemed about a foot square flew off from around the cowling. Just as both the enemy aircraft and myself ran into cloud, he exploded with a terrific flash of flame and black smoke. Immediately after this, my windshield and hood were covered with oil and there was a terrific clatter as pieces of debris struck my aircraft. I broke away hardly able to see through my hood or windshield. My number 2 said he saw a piece about 10ft long break off the enemy aircraft."

The dramatic action had taken

LEFT:
Although achieving some success over Dieppe, Sqn Ldr Johnny Johnson the CO of 610 Squadron considered the Spitfire Vb outclassed.
VIA C F SHORES

OPERATION JUBILEE

him to 'acedom', but damage from the debris forced him to bale out. He was picked up by a boat and then suffered the trauma of being attacked when at sea during which he leaped overboard to save a badly wounded man from a stricken launch.

Withdrawal cover

The air action was to continue for much of the day. The withdrawal commenced at 1100hrs when 124 Squadron's Spitfire VIs saw considerable action that saw victories for Plt Offs Johnnie Hull and Mike Kilburn. Flt Sgt Peter Durnford attacked another FW 190 from 200yds and after his second burst he saw it catch fire and was later confirmed as destroyed. Then he saw a bomber below him: "I saw a Ju 88 flying at 2000 feet. I dived to 300yds range the e/a immediately dived to tree top level. I closed the range to about 250yds and gave a one second burst seeing strikes round the port engine nacelle. After firing the remainder of my cannons, the e/a dropped its bombs. I immediately did a steep climbing turn to the right to about 2000 feet and looking down saw the Ju 88 crash into a field with a dark smoke trail coming from its port engine which had stopped." On return his camera gun showed his victim to have been a Dornier Do 217.

The battles over the coast and the battered flotillas as they withdrew continued through the afternoon resulting in a steady stream of losses and claims. One fell in the early afternoon to Plt Off Sammy Sampson of 602 Squadron who shortly before 1400hrs found himself off Dieppe at 10,000ft: "Two FW 190s appeared no more than 100 yards in front of us, climbing away from the ships and crossing going away to our left. I don't think the Hun pilot saw me for he turned to starboard which enabled me to give me a three second burst from 150yds and he went down on fire to the sea, very close to the ships." Also successful was Flt Lt Eric Bocock who became an ace. Among others, the Norwegians were active again through the afternoon during which 2/Lt Svein Heglund of 331 Squadron began his path to becoming his nation's leading fighter pilot of World War Two when flying Spitfire Vb AR343/FN-A he destroyed a Focke Wulf. Lt Rolf Berg, also of 331 Squadron was also in action. Flying BL579/FN-B he damaged an FW 190 and before being forced to bale out. Fortunately, he was rescued by the launch ML190 and landed at Newhaven.

In mid-afternoon the Tangmere Wing led by Wg Cdr Pat Gibbs in EP120/SD-Y (of 502 Squadron) flew out to escort the homeward bound shipping carrying the troops that had been evacuated from Dieppe. There were several contacts and Gibbs spotted three Do 217s as they broke cloud. He chased one, opening fire at 500 yards and saw many hits before the Dornier suddenly lost speed as one of the engines seized. He then turned to counter an attack from FW 190s as Sgt Tommy de Courcey from 118 Sqn flying Spitfire Vb EP130/NK-Y finished off the crippled bomber. Another Dornier fell to Flt Lt John Shepherd, also of 118 Squadron. The action over the ships continued well into the evening with one of the final actions being conducted by Wg Cdr Michael Pedley's 131 Squadron during which he shared in the destruction of a Junkers Ju 88 with Fg Offs Copeland and Jackson.

It had been the greatest air battle of World War Two, but 62 Spitfires and 29 pilots had been lost. Interestingly, Wg Cdr Gibbs' aircraft survived the war and remains flying from Duxford as a warbird. Sqn Ldr Johnnie Johnson, later the most successful Spitfire pilot of the war, concluded: "Our Spitfire Vs were completely outclassed by the FW 190s and on this occasion I was certainly lucky to get back."

ABOVE: This Spitfire Vb coded HL-C of the 308th FS seen at Kenley in July 1942 is fitted with an early pattern 'blunt' spinner and was flown by Capt Frank Hill. AUTHOR'S COLLECTION

BELOW: Maj Harrison Thyng, the CO of the USAAF 309th FS claimed a 'probable' victory over Dieppe. VIA J SCUTTS

Debut at Dieppe

Given the overall disaster of Operation Jubilee the fact that the North American Mustang had its combat debut at Dieppe is often overlooked.

The task of providing air cover whilst monitoring the approaches to Dieppe for German reinforcements was given to 35 Wing of Army Co-operation Command which comprised four squadrons of Mustang Is fitted with oblique cameras for the reconnaissance role. One of these was 414 Squadron under Wg Cdr Roy Begg, the squadron was based at Croydon and the operation would be its combat debut. With Operation Jubilee planned for August 19, on the previous day the squadron was put onto standby and later in the day the CO and the flight commanders flew to Gatwick to be briefed on the unit's tasks.

Dawn task

Operations for 414 Squadron began at 0445hrs as the landing forces were approaching the French coast. Mustang I AG655/RU-X flown by Flt Lt Freddie Clarke with Fg Off Hollis Hills in AG612/RU-B as 'weaver' to give cover took off. They flew a tactical reconnaissance of the St Valery-Dondeville-Bacqueville area but saw nothing significant before returning to base, landing at 0620hrs. Hills later recalled the sortie: "On the pitch-black morning of 19 August 1942, Flt Lt Freddie Clarke and I, as weaver, took off from Gatwick for a road recce from Abbeville to Dieppe, checking for movement of German armour. How I was able to find Freddie in the dark I'll never know. There were no navigation lights, and the join up was on the deck. I was stepped up on Freddie as we flew across the Channel just a few feet above the water. About halfway across station keeping on Freddie's plane was made easy by the glow of AA fire and searchlights at Dieppe, where Bostons were attacking the heavy guns. As soon as we crossed the coast, however, I lost sight of Freddie in the inky black and I had to finish the mission alone. I could make out nothing on the ground – no roads, no vehicle tracks, nothing." That result was to be typical of the day.

The second pair of Flt Lt Jack Amos (in AM160/RU-T) and Fg Off Ray MacQuaid (AG582) left at 0500hrs and reconnoitred from Dieppe to Blange-Neuchatel-St Victor-Longueville returning at 0630hrs. As they touched down, Plt Off David Bernhardt flying AG376/RU-R and Plt Off Stuart Chapman in AG470/RU-M took off to cover the area between Longrey and Haute Forêt but again saw little of interest. They landed at 0735hrs. By then Plt Off George Burroughs (AG444/RU-Y) and Fg Off F H Chesters (AG375/RU-F) were airborne and covered the roads leading to Dieppe from St Leger-Gauville-Amiens before returning shortly before 0800hrs. Almost an hour before this Fg Off Cliff Horncastle (AG459) and Plt Off Charles 'Smokey' Stover (AG601) took off to cover the same approaches to Dieppe as the previous pair, though it was somewhat more eventful. While flying at low altitude 25 miles into France they were jumped by FW 190s. Horncastle saw them coming and managed to get on the tail of one for about five minutes but, as luck would have it, only one of his guns fired. About the

> **Operations for 414 Squadron began at 0445hrs as the landing forces were approaching the French coast**

BELOW: For the tactical reconnaissance role, the Mustang Is of 414 Squadron were fitted with an oblique camera fitted on the port side aft of the cockpit, visible in this view of AG527/RU-H.
DND/RCAF

OPERATION JUBILEE

RIGHT: During his only sortie to Dieppe, Fg Off Cliff Horncastle was intercepted by FW 190s that he evaded though his aircraft was damaged when it struck a bird. DND/RCAF

same time four more FW 190s dived down and Horncastle broadcast a warning to his wingman. Stover took violent evasive action during which the wingtip of his Mustang struck a telegraph pole as he later recalled: "There was a crash, the next thing I knew I'd left four feet of wing behind me. I sure wasted no time getting out of that place." With part of the wing including half the aileron missing, only with considerable flying skill was Stover able to bring his aircraft back to a successful crash landing but commented later: "I guess I was pretty sore for a while. After all, Holly got a Jerry. But boy, it would have been nice to make it two." Fg Off Horncastle also returned, though having evaded the FW 190 his aircraft hit a bird at low level that left a hole in the starboard wing.

Plt Off Champlin (AM160/RU-T) covered by Flt Lt Sanderson (AG655/RU-X) then flew a gun laying sortie, landing shortly after 0900hrs. By now the withdrawal had been ordered and was being conducted under heavy fire from coastal gun batteries. Therefore, at 0930hrs a further pair of Mustangs took off. Plt Off 'Chick' Davidson in AG582 and AG612/RU-B flown by Plt Off Bill Blakeney were on a special sortie to locate the positions of guns that were firing on the Royal Navy ships offshore that were covering the withdrawal from the Dieppe beaches.

Significant combat

The gun spotting sortie landed at 1040hrs but 15 minutes earlier Flt Lt Freddie Clarke in AG375/RU-F again with Fg Off Hollis Hills flying AG470/RU-M as weaver had left on another road reconnaissance. During the transit to France, Hill's radio became unserviceable, and he was unable to communicate with Clarke's aircraft. This loss had significant

BELOW: Plt Off 'Smokey' Stover ruefully examines the starboard wing of his Mustang that had several feet torn off when evading an FW 190. DND/RCAF

> *How I was able to find Freddie in the dark I'll never know. There were no navigation lights, and the join up was on the deck*

results when Hills spotted some FW 190s as he later described: "As we approached the French coast, the sky was full of fighters in one massive dogfight. A couple of miles short of landfall I spotted four FW 190s off to our right at about 1,500ft. Their course and speed was going to put them directly overhead when we crossed the beach. I called a 'tally ho!' When Freddie turned right to intercept our recce road at Abbeville, we were put in an ideal position for the FWs to attack. I swung very wide dusting the Abbeville chimney tops. That kept me beneath the FWs. The lead FW 190 hit Freddie's Mustang with the first burst. I got a long range shot at the FW leader but had to break right when his number two man had a go at me and made a big mistake of sliding to my left side ahead of me. It was an easy shot and I hit him hard. His engine caught fire, and soon after it started smoking and the canopy came off. I hit him again and he was a goner, falling off to the right into the trees." Hollis Hills had achieved the first ever victory for the Mustang. He continued: "The second pair of FW 190s had vanished so I raced towards Dieppe looking for Freddie's Mustang. I saw him heading for the harbour at 1,000 feet, streaming glycol, with the lead FW trailing behind. The FW started to slide dead astern Freddie, so I gave him a short high deflection burst to get his attention. He broke hard left into my attack and the ensuing fight seemed to go on forever. I could out turn him, very slowly gaining an advantage, but just as I got into firing position he would break off and streak inland,

using the superior power of his BMW engine. He would come back at me as soon as I turned to head for the coast, and we'd start our turning competition all over again. During one turn I had to dodge a crashing plane – a Bf 109 – and the FW pilot got his only shot at me. His deflection was too great, and he missed. My opponent was a highly competent pilot, and I was ready to call a draw as soon as I could."

Clarke's Mustang had been hit with a burst of fire from an FW 190, possibly that flown by Oltn Zink of 2./JG 26. Freddie Clarke, who had been slightly injured in the hand, managed to ditch his Mustang offshore, cracking his forehead on the gunsight. He was picked up by a passing landing craft then passed onto the destroyer HMS *Calpe*. He returned to England safely where he submitted his combat report: "We crossed the French coast at St Aubin sur Mer, and I picked up the road which was my task and had followed it in behind Dieppe. Then I was jumped by a Focke Wulf 190 which shot my oil and glycol cooler away. I immediately turned tight left and three-quarters of the way round turn I saw that my oil pressure was nil. My engine started to seize. I immediately straightened out, used my excess speed to gain height to about 800ft and headed for the sea off Dieppe. Just before straightening out, on my port rear quarter I saw a FW 190 with grey smoke pouring from it heading towards a wood apparently out of control. In my opinion it was impossible for the pilot to do anything but pile up in the wood."

At 1130hrs, ten minutes before Hills had landed Flt Lt Jack Amos in AM160/RU-T and Fg Off Ray MacQuoid in AG582 took off from Gatwick for the squadron's final recce sortie of Operation Jubilee. The pair covered the area of Tourville-Cleres-Cailly-Torny, but MacQuoid's aircraft was hit by flak forcing him to abandon the sortie. When they landed at 1230hrs they brought 414 Squadron's participation in the Dieppe operation to a close. In all, 414 Squadron had flown 18 tactical reconnaissance sorties to the French coast but had seen no military movement though heavy flak was encountered on most flights. However, the squadron had given the Mustang its operational debut and achieved the type's first air combat victory.

ABOVE: During the penultimate sortie of Operation Jubilee, Plt Off Hollis Hills' section was intercepted by FW 190s, one of which he shot down to claim the Mustang's first victory. DND/RCAF

BELOW: Mustang I AG375/RU-F was 414 Squadron's only loss during Dieppe when it was damaged by an FW 190 and forced to ditch. F E CLARKE VIA N FRANKS

THE DESTINATION FOR AVIATION ENTHUSIASTS

Visit us today and discover all our publications

FlyPast is internationally regarded as the magazine for aviation history and heritage.

Aeroplane is still providing the best aviation coverage around, with focus on iconic military aircraft from the 1930s to the 1960s.

SIMPLY SCAN THE QR CODE OF YOUR FAVOURITE TITLE ABOVE TO FIND OUT MORE!

FREE P&P* when you order

shop.keypublishing.com

Call **+44 (0)1780 480404** *(Mon to Fri 9am - 5.30pm GMT)*

SUBSCRIBE TODAY!

Aviation News is renowned for providing the best coverage of every brand of aviation.

Airforces Monthly is devoted to modern military aircraft and their air arms.

from our online shop...
/collections/subscriptions

*Free 2nd class P&P on all UK & BFPO orders. Overseas charges apply.

REGENSBURG AND SCHWEINFURT DEEP PENETRATION DISASTER

Needing to crush Messerschmitt fighter production, US bomber crews fought a savage gun battle high over Germany.

WORDS: TOM ALLETT

In its pursuit of bombing accuracy, the US strategy of flying close formation, high altitude, daylight raids ensured bloody battles would take place whatever the target within mainland Europe. The deeper the penetration into Nazi-held airspace, the greater the risk to the bomber crews. While fighter escorts could provide an element of protection for the attacking force, once the escorts' fuel tanks dictated a return to base, the bombers were on their own. Only the concentrated defensive fire of the tightly boxed formations could provide any kind of shield against the Luftwaffe fighters' onslaught but, conversely, the bombers' close proximity to each other made them more vulnerable to the shrapnel of the high-reaching flak guns. This scenario was never more costly than during the now infamous double-strike raid against the military production factories at Regensburg and Schweinfurt in the summer of 1943.

Background

Seeking to minimise the loss of men and machines during bombing raids deep into Germany, the United States Army Air Force (USAAF)'s mission planners devised a strategy to use Allied air bases in North Africa. During what became known as the shuttle raids, after striking their targets, instead of returning to their bases in England, the bombers would continue south, across the Mediterranean Sea to land at Allied-held airfields in North Africa. The surviving bomber crews would still have to run the gauntlet of flak and fighters when tasked with a bombing raid in the opposite direction some days later but, in theory, refreshed, rearmed, and refuelled their survival odds were greater than they would be when facing defending fighters, unescorted, for twice as long during the same raid.

The first shuttle raid was supposed to deliver a crushing blow against the Nazi's aircraft production capabilities by attacking the Messerschmitt 109

BELOW: The Luftwaffe flew the Messerschmitt Bf 109 in greater numbers than any other fighter, hence the targeting on the Regensburg production facilities.
BUNDESARCHIV

production lines at Regensberg and the ball bearing factories at Schweinfurt. In 1943, both targets were well beyond the range of Allied escort fighters but this time they would be aided by a new 'double strike' tactic – separate large bomber formations attacking two targets during the same raid – that could increase the bomber crews' chances of success. The theory was attacking two targets during the same raid would bring confusion to the Luftwaffe's fighter controllers' decisions making while simultaneously dividing the defending fighter force between two locations.

Battle order: 1943

In the summer of 1943, the Allied leaders drew up the Pointblank Directive. It sought to coordinate RAF and USAAF bombing operations against German aircraft production. The Pointblank Directive ultimately became Operation Pointblank, which was tasked with severely restricting the effectiveness of the Luftwaffe's fighter force in preparation for the inevitable Allied invasion of Europe, whenever that would take place.

After America's post-Pearl Harbor entry into World War Two, the first USAAF Eighth Air Force bomber crews arrived at their English bases in July 1942. However, that November, Operation Torch, the Allies' invasion of North Africa, required some of the American bombers to be relocated to that theatre, leaving only six USAAF Bomb Groups in England: four equipped with B-17 Flying Fortresses and two flying the B-24 Liberator. This relatively small force was clearly inadequate for the ambition of Pointblank and the B-17 element was rapidly quadrupled in strength. Initially known as the 1st and 3rd Bombardment Wings, their expansion led to their redesignation as Bomb Divisions. The Americans suffered significant losses during Pointblank raids against Focke Wulf aircraft factories in Bremen, Kassel, and Oschersleben but enough bomb damage was achieved to deem the attacks successful. The factories building Messerschmitt 109s – Regensburg in southeast Germany and Wiener Neustadt, in Austria – being much further away, represented a far more challenging target. Nevertheless, given they delivered almost half of German fighter production, they simply had to be destroyed.

First attempt

The first Pointblank attempt to smash the Messerschmitt factories was disrupted by poor weather. UK-based B-17s of the USAAF Eighth Air Force (8AF) were detailed to attack Regensburg while North Africa-based B-24s of the Ninth Air Force (9AF) would strike Weiner Neustadt. The original raid was set for August 7, 1943, but the weather forced its complete cancellation. A second ▶

ABOVE:
This image, dated August 17, 1943, was taken from 42-5861 *Laden Maiden*, **shows B-17Fs 42-3393** *Just-ASnappin* **(far right), 42-3237** *Stymie* **(top), 42-30061** *Wolff Pack* **and 42-30066** *Mugwump* **heading for North Africa following a strike on the Messerschmitt factory in the southeast German city of Regensburg.**
100TH BOMB GROUP FOUNDATION.

REGENSBURG AND SCHWEINFURT

ABOVE: Colonel Curtis LeMay, who would go on to lead the August 1943 attack on the Messerschmitt factories at Regensburg, is seen congratulating a B-17 crew of the 306th Bomb Group at Chelveston airfield in June 1942. USAF

attempt was set for August 13. This time the 9AF Liberators did make their attack, albeit with only limited success, but the 8AF remained 'weathered in' in England.

A new date, August 17, was chosen and the raid plan was named Mission 84. This would involve a second new tactic, the recently employed 'shuttle' element, plus what became known as the USAAF's 'double strike' method. The B-17s of the 3rd Bombardment Wing (3BW), equipped with the so-called 'Tokyo' long-range fuel tanks would lead the way. Their target would be the Messerschmitt Bf109 factories in Regensburg before flying on to airfields in French Algeria. The 1st Bombardment Wing (1BW) would follow close behind 3BW but, before reaching Regensburg, it would swing northeast and strike the ball-bearing factories at Schweinfurt while, hopefully, many of the Luftwaffe fighters were on the ground refuelling and rearming.

Remarkably, almost all of Nazi Germany's ball-bearing production was grouped in close proximity within the city, so there was an opportunity to severely disrupt supply if the bombing was accurate. After its attack, 1BW would return to its bases in England. Allied fighters could escort the bombers as far as the edge of German airspace but for the next hour the bombers would have to fight their way to their targets alone. The theory was that 3BW would encounter its toughest fight inbound to its target while 1BW would face its biggest battle on the way home. Coordinated timing was going to be all-important.

Diversion tactics

In an attempt to draw the Luftwaffe fighters away from the Regensburg strike two diversionary attacks were arranged. One, comprising USAAF B-26 Marauders and RAF B-25 Mitchell medium bombers, would attack the Luftwaffe-held airfields of Bryas-Sud and Marck as another force of Mitchells attacked railway marshalling yards at Dunkirk. Each was intended to coincide with the Regensburg attack. In a separate effort RAF Hawker Typhoons would attack the Luftwaffe bases at Lille-Vendeville, Poix, and

RIGHT: B-17s over Schweinfurt, note the smoke from the bomb bursts, partially obscured by clouds. USAF

RIGHT:
In Regensburg, all six of the main Messerschmitt factories were hit and either severely damaged or destroyed. BUNDESARCHIV

BELOW:
The recently introduced 'shuttle' tactic required the bombers from the Regensburg force to fly south, over the Alps, ultimately landing at Allied-held airfields in North Africa. USAF

Woensdrecht, with USAAF B-26s delivering a second strike against Poix as the Schweinfurt formations were returning.

As always, coordination was vital. The bomber formations would take up to two hours to climb to their operating altitude while assembling into their tight battle formations before flying into enemy airspace. The Regensburg mission would last about 11 hours so, even when planning a dawn departure (on this occasion that would be 0630hrs British Double Summer Time - DBST) there was only 90-minutes of leeway to launch the 3BW B-17s if they were to land at the North African airfields in daylight.

Delay at dawn

Combat flying always places a heavy burden on the participants' nerves so imagine the tension at dawn on August 17, 1943. Fog covered the bomber bases in East Anglia postponing take-off until 0800hrs, the latest permissible without cancelling the raid.

The bomber crews were well aware that this deep penetration raid was going to involve a prolonged battle and some of them would not be coming back; no doubt a few quiet prayers were said as the 'go-no go' decision was awaited. The fog gradually dissipated, allowing the Regensburg force to take-off, but not the Schweinfurt crews. The plan had begun to unravel even before 1BW had started its engines. Despite a coordinated Regensburg and Schweinfurt attack being deemed critical to the mission's chances of minimising aircraft losses the Regensburg force was already reaching the Dutch coast by the time the Schweinfurt bombers were taking to the air. The gap now forming between the two waves of bombers would enable the Luftwaffe fighters to refuel and rearm in time to engage the Schweinfurt crews. To counter this threat, the Schweinfurt force's take-off was further delayed enabling the Allied fighters covering the first part of the Regensburg force's journey to return to their UK bases and replenish their supplies before repeating their task in support of the Schweinfurt (1BW) force. The gap between the two mission waves was now more than three hours, the coordination aspect of Mission 84 was lost and the threat facing the bomber crews was now greater than ever.

Regensburg force

Colonel Curtiss LeMay led the Regensburg strike force.

REGENSBURG AND SCHWEINFURT

He had already played a role in forming USAAF bombing policy but, leading from the front, the next few hours would cement his place in air force combat history.

His Regensburg force comprised seven B-17 Groups totalling 146 aircraft. All but one of the groups formed a 21-aircraft combat box tactical formation with the groups formed into three large formations known as Provisional Combat Wings. Three groups in 'Vee' formation wing boxes (sometimes casually referred to as a 'staggered formation') led the way, followed by two wing boxes of two groups in echelon formation, the second of which would trail its leader at a slightly lower altitude. Luftwaffe fighters fell upon the Regensburg-bound B-17s just 15 minutes after crossing the Dutch coast at 1000hrs, by which time the last formation of bombers was about 15 miles behind the leaders. Instead of being able to contribute to the mutual defensive machine gun fire possible with close formation flying, they were not even able to see each other, and the intensity of the fighter attacks continued to grow.

Two groups of Republic P-47 Thunderbolts comprising 87 aircraft had been tasked with accompanying the Regensburg formation as far as their range would allow, essentially the German border. The first group of P-47s arrived as per the arranged rendezvous plan and took up their position around the lead wing but the second group arrived some 15 minutes late and the rear section of the Regensburg force received no fighter protection at all. Although the P-47s' presence probably did cause some Luftwaffe fighters to hold off their attacks until after the American escort fighters turned for home, none of the P-47s were able to engage their enemy and put any of the Luftwaffe defenders out of the fight. The German fighters' attacks continued relentlessly for around 90 minutes before they had to break off to refuel and rearm. By

ABOVE:
B-17Fs seen during the Schweinfurt mission. USAF

BELOW:
Bomb bursts at Regensburg. USAF

70 GREAT AIR BATTLES OF WORLD WAR TWO

www.key.aero

ABOVE: B-17 assigned to the 457th BG in dense flak during a raid against the ball-bearing production plants at Schweinfurt, Germany in 1944. US bomber crews often said the flak they encountered was 'so thick that you could walk on it'. ALAMY

then, 15 B-17s had been shot down or severely damaged, 13 of which were from the trailing formation. Finally, the surviving bombers made it to Regensburg where their crews described the anti-aircraft fire (flak) as 'light' and the visibility 'clear'. The first bombs fell at 1143hrs DBST with 126 crews subsequently recording 299 tons of bombs released upon the city's Messerschmitt factories.

Its job done; the Regensburg force turned south, aiming to cross the Alps en route for North Africa. This 'shuttle' move – heading away from their UK bases – took the Germans by surprise and only a handful of twin-engined Messerschmitt Bf110s were able to engage the Africa-bound Fortresses. Two damaged B-17s left the Regensburg formation to make forced landings in neutral Switzerland where their crews were interred but Curtis LeMay, still leading the force, ordered his crews to make two wide orbits in Swiss airspace, taking up around ten minutes, which allowed some stragglers to rejoin the main formation before it turned for Africa. One Regensburg B-17 crashed in Italy and five more were forced to ditch in the Mediterranean Sea after running out of fuel. Overall, 24 bombers from the Regensburg force were lost and, of the 122 B-17s that made it to Tunisia, more than 60 had suffered battle damage. Despite the long-running carnage of the preceding hours, the Luftwaffe was ready and able to meet the Schweinfurt force that followed.

Destination Schweinfurt

The Schweinfurt force, comprising nine B-17 Groups, was led by 41-year-old Texan, Brigadier General Robert B Williams. Like Colonel Le May, Williams had already played a significant role in developing US bombing strategy before leading from the front in what would become one of the most tragic days in USAAF history. Williams was among the first service pilots to fly the B-17, having been posted to handle the then Army Air Corps first examples, received in 1937. Prior to America's entry into the war, he was sent to London to observe the attacks being made on southeast England. On one occasion, instead

> ❝ On one occasion, instead of heading for the shelters, he chose to watch an air raid from the roof of his hotel resulting in him losing an eye to shrapnel ❞

of heading for the shelters, he chose to watch an air raid from the roof of his hotel resulting in him losing an eye to shrapnel. He didn't let it hinder his flying career, returning to fly as soon as the opportunity arose. It is fair to say his rise through the air force ranks was meteoric, even by wartime standards, and his 'lead from the front' approach had won profound respect among his peers. He didn't have to lead the Schweinfurt raid, but he chose to.

To achieve a 'maximum effort' against Schweinfurt, 1BW sent 230 B-17s, composed of 12 groups, divided into two task forces, each with two wings. Each wing was composed of a three-group formation and in total stretched over 20 miles. Williams led the mission while flying as co-pilot in a B-17 within the lead formation.

The Schweinfurt B-17s followed the same course as the Regensburg force but it was now many hours behind the intended schedule. A rearranged fighter escort was quickly assembled comprising 96 RAF Spitfires which would shepherd the bombers as far as the Antwerp area before USAAF P-47s would take over the escort role until almost the German border when they too would need to turn for home.

The bombers planned to fly at altitudes of between 23,000– ▶

REGENSBURG AND SCHWEINFURT

ABOVE: The Schweinfurt force, comprising nine B-17 Groups, was led by 41-year-old Texan, Brigadier General Robert B Williams. USAF

26,500ft but as they approached the Dutch coast at about 1330hrs they encountered developing cloud masses that had not been forecast or present when the Regensburg force passed that way several hours earlier. The clouds appeared to be towering beyond the B-17s' achievable altitude, forcing the bombers to descend to around 17,000ft, making them more vulnerable to fighters and flak. Again, the Luftwaffe fighters attacked shortly after the bombers had crossed the coast, subjecting them to a series of head-on attacks. The Spitfire escort engaged the attacking Messerschmitt 109s and Focke Wulf 190s, claiming eight as destroyed, but the fuel burnt in combat forced the RAF fighters to return to base earlier than originally hoped. Their replacement, 88 P-47s spilt into two groups, arrived several minutes late, providing the German fighters with their first 'window of opportunity' to attack without harassment from Allied fighters. Despite their late arrival, the P-47s did engage in some combats, but their fuel levels soon forced them to return to base too. The bombers were now alone over Germany and about to face the sternest opposition.

Rockets

The bombers were about to encounter a new weapon, unguided rockets which had recently been trialled on day and night fighters. The Messerschmitt Bf 109Gs of the Luftwaffe's 5 Staffel/JG11 had introduced them to service only 24 hours earlier and would now fire them in anger against the American raiders. They were not alone with this new weaponry as the Luftwaffe, unusually for this stage of the war, also deployed rocket-firing Bf 110 night-fighters to this daytime battle. The rockets were relatively inaccurate in terms of aiming, but when launched against tightly packed bombers there was a significant chance of success. Whatever their performance, the rockets were certainly a terrifying sight for the bomber crews who saw them. Overall, the Luftwaffe committed more than 300 fighters to this long-running battle. Although the original time schedule and 'double strike' element of the mission had been discarded due to a series of delays, just after 1430hrs the B-17s changed course for Schweinfurt, thereby indicating the force's intended target. Cannon shells smashed into the B-17s as wave after wave of fighter attacks struck home; 22 bombers, along with their 220 crew members, tumbled from the sky. Such heavy losses among the lead elements of the force – before the target had even been reached – led some survivors to later recall they had feared all the bombers might be lost. At one point, raid commander Brigadier General Williams abandoned his copilot's seat, leaving the aircraft's captain to continue flying their B-17 while Williams manned a machine gun, blasting away at the German fighters.

As the lead B-17s reached the outskirts of Schweinfurt, the Luftwaffe fighters broke away to refuel and rearm. Now the city's flak guns were able to fire on the attackers without any fear of hitting their own fighters. Flak brought down three B-17s over Schweinfurt but, just before 1500hrs, the first bombs dropped and the following stream of B-17s took approximately 24 minutes to pass over the target factories.

Smoke billowing from the increasing number of explosions hampered the following crews' efforts to pinpoint their targets but 183 crews recorded dropping 424 tons of bombs before turning for home to face a second onslaught.

The need to maintain formation and concentrate defensive fire was so great that, despite the terrible losses already suffered, some 15 minutes after leaving Schweinfurt and while still over Germany, each of the B-17 groups entered a circular holding pattern to enable the formations to tighten up. As the B-17s headed west towards Brussels and ultimately, home, the Luftwaffe renewed its attacks and 'stragglers' – damaged aircraft that were forced to drop out of formation – were singled out for destruction. A running battle lasted about 50 minutes before the surviving bombers reached the relative sanctuary of an umbrella of more than 180 P-47s and Spitfires that were once again in range. The Allied fighters claimed 21 Luftwaffe machines shot down although eight more B-17s were also lost before reaching the North Sea and a further three were forced to ditch in it. Thirty-six B-17s from the Schweinfurt force were shot down during its ordeal.

Analysis

Post war analysis reveals the Regensburg – Schweinfurt 'double strike' raid of August 17, 1943, as among the USAAF's costliest days of the war in Europe. Disasters are never the result of a single problem; they are the product of a series of elements combining to deliver a devastating result. The B-17 crews had faced a series of problems, fog, towering cloud formations, unfamiliar tactics, missed rendezvous, and new

> **" The theory was attacking two targets during the same raid would bring confusion to the Luftwaffe's fighter controllers "**

weapons, the end result being 60 bombers and 552 crew members lost. Thankfully not all were killed, about half became prisoners of war and 20 men were interned after landing in neutral Switzerland. Five crews were rescued after ditching at sea but, inside aircraft that made it back to base, seven men were fatally wounded, and 21 others injured. The 1BW spent approximately 3.5 hours over Germany, of which about 2hrs 10mins was completely without fighter support. The 60 bombers downed was more than double the highest number previously lost on a single raid up until that point and more than 50 others were damaged, some of them beyond repair. Several of the Regensburg machines that arrived damaged in North Africa were simply abandoned. Escort fighter losses were thankfully few, with just three P-47s and two Spitfires shot down. Allied fighters claimed 32 Luftwaffe 'kills' while the bomber gunners claimed an astonishing 288 fighters shot down. Post war analysis of Luftwaffe records reveal no more than 27 German fighters were lost.

The bombing analysis made better reading. In Regensburg, all six of the main Messerschmitt factories were hit and either severely damaged or destroyed. Less structural damage was achieved at Schweinfurt, but it was still significant with the two largest ball-bearing factories suffering around 80 direct hits and many of the other factories suffered significant fire damage due to the use of incendiary bombs. German records state 203 civilians were killed in the Schweinfurt attack.

Albert Speer, Nazi-Germany's minister of armaments and war, reported an immediate 34% drop in ball-bearing production but believed the shortfall was quickly rectified from surpluses drawn from around the country. Speer told post-war investigators he felt the USAAF made two major mistakes during the Schweinfurt raid. The first was dividing its strength between two targets instead concentrating all its might against the ball-bearing plants; the second was its failure to immediately follow-up the August 17 strike.

The results of the Regensburg – Schweinfurt 'double strike' underlined the folly of deep penetration raids that stretched well beyond the range of escort fighters; the losses were simply not sustainable. Inevitably, Schweinfurt would have to be raided again. The lessons of the first raid had not been learned and when a second attack took place on October 14, the losses were similar. More than 20% of the attacking force was lost, resulting in the suspension of deep penetration raids until the long-range North American Mustangs came into service five months later. In the annals of US warfare, the Regensburg and Schweinfurt raids serve as reminders of the courage required – and cost to be borne – to win wars. ■

> **In an attempt to draw the Luftwaffe fighters away from the Regensburg strike two diversionary attacks were arranged**

ABOVE: With coordination between the Regensburg and Schweinfurt attacks completely lost, the Luftwaffe fighters were refuelled and rearmed in time to meet the Schweinfurt raiders. BUNDESARCHIV

BELOW: A B-17 nicknamed *High Life* of the 100th Bomb Group that crash landed in Switzerland, where aircraft and crew were interned. USAF

GREAT AIR BATTLES OF WORLD WAR TWO 73

LUFTWAFFE AIRCRAFT OF WORLD WAR TWO

The Junkers Ju-87 played a significant part in the Battle of Britain's 'Hardest Day' — August 18, 1940 — attacking airfields on England's south coast. This Stuka B-2 T6+HL flew with 3./StG 2, the dive bomber group named 'Immelmann' from the Luftwaffe held airfield at St Malo, France. ALL PROFILES ANDY HAY-FLYINGART

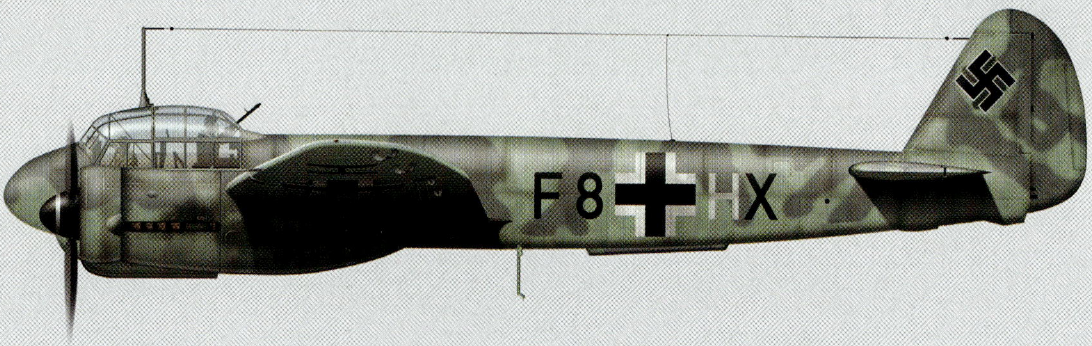

The Luftwaffe made famously negligible impact during D-Day itself although it did belatedly increase its presence over the Normandy beaches when it was effectively too late to affect the Allies' momentum. The Luftwaffe's shortage of aircraft on the western front is partially illustrated in this image of Ju 88C6 F8+HX of Kg40. Previously a night fighter unit, it was transferred to day combat duties in a forlorn attempt to restore parity of numbers against its RAF and USAAF opponents.

The Messerschmitt Bf 109 formed the backbone of the Luftwaffe's fighter force throughout World War Two. The Bf 109G model illustrated here was the most prevalent variant in service during the hard-fought battles over Regensburg and Schweinfurt in 1943.

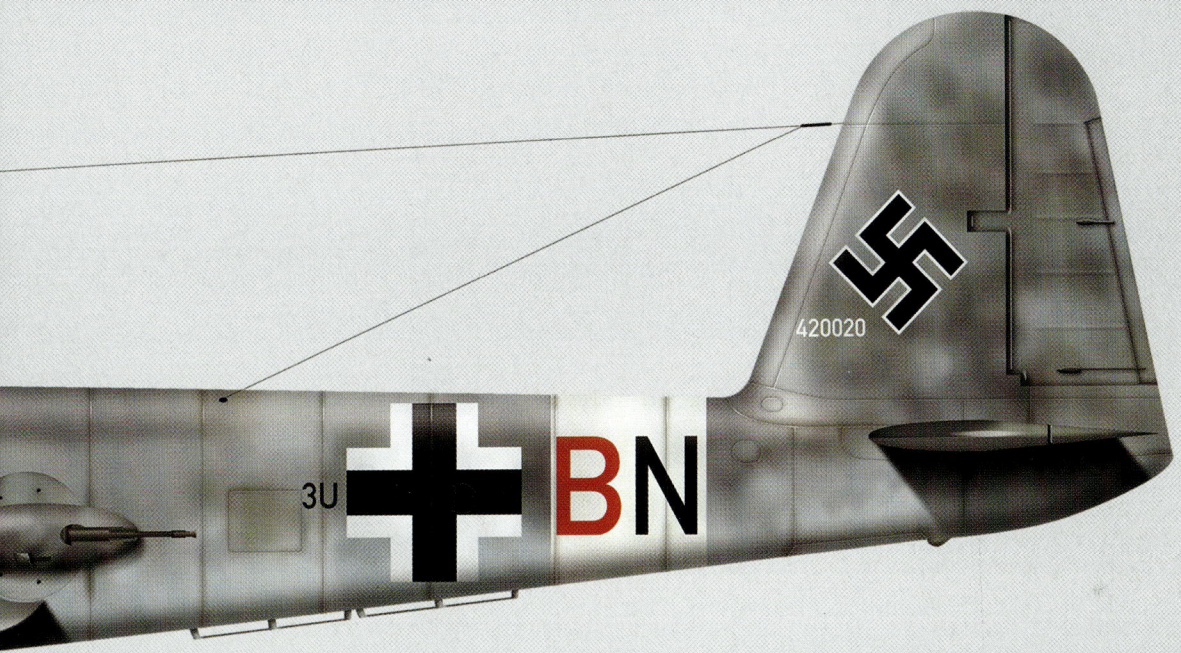

In its increasingly intensive daytime battles against US heavy bomber formations the Luftwaffe began to introduce more heavily armed twin-engined fighters such as the Messerschmitt Me 410. The variant shown here is a Me 410 B1 3U+BN of 5.ZG26, a rare 'bomber destroyer' example equipped with a 50mm cannon. Its firepower was devastating enough to destroy an aircraft with only one or two hits.

Fw 190 A-8 'Blue 9' was flown by Lt Karl-Heinz Koch during the battle over Forde Fjord, Norway, on February 9, 1945. Koch had already scored five victories before the Forde Fjord 'Black Friday' encounter in which he claimed a Mustang destroyed, but he too was shot down immediately afterwards. Koch survived the war.

BIG WEEK

ONE HELL OF AN ARGUMENT

The sheer scale and ferocity of Operation Argument, an all-out attack on Germany's aircraft production capabilities, led it to be remembered as 'Big Week'   **WORDS:** TOM ALLETT

Despite years of attacks on the Nazis' industrial capacity, as late as 1944, their aircraft manufacturing output continued to increase. If the Allied invasion of Europe were to succeed it was imperative that air superiority be achieved over western Europe and that should begin by restricting the Luftwaffe's aircraft supply chain. To achieve this Britain and the United States agreed on the Combined Bomber Offensive (CBO) to coordinate their respective operations against Germany's aircraft production and its associated component suppliers.

In its earliest form the CBO led to the organisation of Operation Pointblank (see page 66) which subsequently became the Pointblank Directive and harmonised the details of what was an 'around the clock' strategy. The USAAF would attack by day while the RAF would continue to strike by night. As Allied preparations for what would become the Normandy landings intensified, so did the attacks on aircraft production facilities.

In the opening weeks of 1944 ideas were drawn up for an intense series of raids which could deliver a knockout blow to Nazi fighter production. The plan was for a week-long campaign against factories in central and southern Germany which would simultaneously provide an opportunity to destroy the Luftwaffe's already operational fighter force. The plan was given the codename Operation Argument with a hoped-for execution in February.

Not everyone agreed that the Pointblank Directive was the best way to try and win the war. There was resistance from RAF Bomber Command's commander-in-chief, Arthur 'Bomber' Harris, who disapproved of what he saw as a dilution of the area bombing campaign he was pursuing. Ultimately though, orders from the then RAF chief of the air staff, Sir Charles Portal, meant Harris had to comply.

The threat

The American bombers, flying in daylight, were exposed to Luftwaffe fighter attacks for the entire time they flew over occupied Europe. For several months, the USAAF had consistently lost just below 2% of its attacking forces. While regrettable from the human point of view, in the brutality of war such numbers were militarily sustainable and 'acceptable' in terms of providing replacement aircraft and crews. However, as the USAAF reached out to attack targets deeper into Germany, the bitter lessons of the 1943 Regensburg and Schweinfurt raids proved how losses

BELOW: UK airshow star *Sally B* is seen when she carried the markings of a 447th Bomb Group aircraft. As part of the USAAF's 8th Air Force the unit was heavily involved in 'Big Week'.
KEY COLLECTION

could quickly reach unsustainable levels when conditions combined against the attackers.

Having achieved such high-scoring successes against the Americans during the Regensburg and Schweinfurt raids the Luftwaffe's leadership believed its tactic of using heavily armed twin-engined fighters such as the Messerschmitt Bf 110 and Me 410 was paying dividends. Work to further improve these so-called bomber destroyers continued through the winter of 1943/44, largely through adding heavier armament, but the US fighters were proving to be deadly opponents when their range enabled them to reach the enemy. The Luftwaffe's initial response was to pull its fighters back to Germany out of the range of Allied fighters but the USAAF's introduction of the long-range Rolls-Royce Merlin equipped P-51 Mustangs delivered a huge advantage to the American raiders. Now the bombers no longer had to fight alone for part of their journey; they could be escorted all the way to their targets and back. Nevertheless, while the tide of war was moving in favour of the Allies, the Luftwaffe still represented a serious threat having more than 2,000 fighters available to defend Germany. US bombing raids were often intercepted by several hundred fighters along their route and – if Allied intelligence were correct – the Axis factories could deliver as many as 3,000 new aircraft per month. That was more than enough to keep pace with Luftwaffe losses, although the difficulty of training enough new pilots to the required standard would gradually weaken the Nazis' defences.

Although the previous year's attacks against major factories at Leipzig, Weiner Neustadt, and Regensburg – all Messerschmitt 109 production facilities – had achieved some damage, those raids were not followed-up quickly enough and full production was always quickly restored.

Strategy

The Americans, now confident their long-range fighters gave them an advantage over the Luftwaffe, even when deep into Germany, believed the Argument raids should aim to draw as many German fighters into the air as possible and destroy them. The theory was that if the raids went unchallenged the bombers would simply destroy their targets unopposed, while if the Luftwaffe did engage – as it surely must – it would be met by the long-range USAAF fighters. To further their effectiveness, the US fighters would be relieved of their usual close escort duties, freeing them to better engage the Luftwaffe machines.

The 'draw them up then shoot them down' strategy was high risk as both the Luftwaffe during the Battle of Britain (1940), and RAF Fighter Command during its offensive actions over occupied Europe from 1941 onwards, had taken similar approaches only to lose more of their own aircraft than they destroyed.

Preparation

Detailed planning fell to the then newly formed US Strategic Air Forces in Europe (USSAFiE) group, established in early 1944. Its deputy commander, General Frederick Anderson, was an experienced combat pilot who already held the US Silver Star for leading bombing raids over Germany. Andreson was confident coordinated attacks could succeed while acknowledging the cost in terms of aircraft and men would be very high.

Although many large-scale raids had already taken place, Operation Argument was going to be the biggest yet and avoid the mistakes of the past by delivering repeated coordinated attacks upon the aircraft factories in a week-long campaign. The USSAFiE strategists recognised the potential losses of their risky strategy could mean losing as much as 18% of their attacking force – way above the 5% regarded as being a replenishable number – acceptable under these exceptional circumstances if the aircraft factories could be wrecked. However, General Anderson thought it may cost 75% of the 981 attacking bombers (736 aircraft and more than 7,000 men) over the week-long operation but he still thought the raids should go ahead. Allied intelligence gathering channels sought every shred of information about the enemy's aircraft, component, and engine manufacturing sites but, even holding the necessary target information, success would also require a week-long spell of reasonable weather. Medium and high-level cloud layers above England would not present a significant problem ▶

ABOVE: Big Week opened with the RAF night attack on Leipzig. Apart from the destruction caused, the German anti-aircraft defences would still be suffering from fatigue the following day when the USAAF hit. KEY COLLECTION

LEFT: The USAAF's General Anderson thought the week-long campaign may cost 75% of the 981 available American bombers (equal to 736 aircraft and more than 7,000 men) but he still believed the raids should go ahead. USAF

BIG WEEK

so long as the visibility was good enough to enable the bombers for join formation before setting course for enemy held airspace, but the skies over the target areas must be clear. This would obviously be a rare occurrence over northern Europe in February. The attacking force would have to be ready to go as soon as the weather forecasts predicted an opportunity, giving the bomber and fighter squadrons only one day's notice to coordinate their many requirements. A suitable 'weather window' was forecast for February 20-25, and the decision to attack was made, but unsuitable weather would repeatedly affect the week's operations causing major implications for 'Argument's' effectiveness.

Battle order

The chosen aircraft production facilities were at Augsburg (aircraft assembly works), Brunswick (engine manufacturing), Gotha and Leipzig (both aircraft assembly factories), Schweinfurt (aircraft assembly), Stuttgart (Daimler-Benz engines) and Steyr, Austria (aero engines and guns). Many Luftwaffe airfields were also targeted.

'Big Week' began with the RAF raid on the Messerschmitt facility at Leipzig during the night of February 19/20. It was a bad start as Bomber Command sent 823 aircraft, losing 78 and suffering 438 aircrew killed, but most of the bombs fell on residential areas and the aircraft factory suffered little damage. The USAAF attacked on the afternoon of the same day and succeeded in causing enough damage to slow the pace of aircraft manufacturing, but the site continued to produce Messerschmitt Bf 109s until the city was captured by Soviet forces the following year. Weather disrupted all daytime 'Argument' attempts on February 21, leaving bombers to attack secondary targets but the RAF's night strike against Stuttgart was more successful. Unlike some other major German cities Stuttgart had escaped major bomb damage but the night of February 21/22 marked a devastating change in the city's fortunes. Bomber Command sent 598 bombers to strike the city with the Daimler-Benz

ABOVE: The USAAF image shows smoke billowing from the Luftwaffe airfield of Diepholz, (marked with an arrow by the wartime photographic interpreter) in south central Germany. The destruction of aircraft factories was 'Big Week's' primary objective, but numerous airfields were also attacked to destroy Luftwaffe aircraft on the ground. USAF

LEFT: The Luftwaffe losses were particularly high amongst its twin-engined Zerstörer units including those flying the Messerschmitt Me 410 'Hornet'. MIKE FREER

ABOVE:
The long-range capability of the North American Mustang was a real 'game changer' in that it enabled the USAAF's daylight bombing raids to be escorted all the way to their targets and back. USAF

engine plant being their central aiming point. Two diversionary raids were staged simultaneously, helping to distract the night defences' efforts very successfully and only eight bombers were lost.

If the USAAF's raids of February 21 were disappointing, an intended US attack against the Gotha factory on February 22 turned into a disaster when cloud cover forced the American bombers to seek alternative targets while returning from Germany. The railway station at the Nazi-occupied Dutch city of Nijmegen was the chosen alternate but the poor bombing pattern killed about 880 Dutch civilians while leaving the railway station almost unscathed. More than 100 additional Dutch civilian casualties were also suffered during the attempted bombing of German-held targets in the Dutch towns of Arnhem, Deventer, and Enschede and many hundreds were made homeless. All operations for February 23 were cancelled, partly due to bad weather but also to allow for study the operational failures of the previous day.

Major attacks resumed the next day. Once again, the USAAF's attention was focused on Gotha. B-24s would attack the aircraft factory which had been reprieved by bad weather on February 22

RIGHT:
The 15th Air Force flew from bases in southern Italy. Here a 451st Bomb Group B-24 Liberator is seen bombing a German railyard in the month after 'Big Week'. USAF

> **The USAAF would attack by day while the RAF would continue to strike by night**

while B-17s would strike the ball-bearing factories at Schweinfurt.

The experiences of the B-24 Liberator crews from the 392nd Bomb Group during their attack on Gotha perhaps illustrate the ferocity and complexity of the battles as well as any other. Thirty-six crews had attended their general briefing at 0530hrs but on start-up four aircraft developed technical problems which forced them to abort their missions. The remaining 32 B-24s carried a combined total of 384 500lb general purpose bombs and the first was airborne at 0850hrs. Repeated Luftwaffe attacks – described in the unit's records as 'relentless' – involving up to 150 fighters, initially Focke Wulf 190s, and Messerschmitt Bf 109s began as the bombers crossed the coast. The onslaught continued for about 90 minutes, the time taken to reach the target, with the Luftwaffe's heavier twin-engined Messerschmitt Bf 110s, Me 210s and possibly Me 410s joining the fight deeper into German airspace, some using a combination of ▶

BIG WEEK

cannon and rocket fire. For part of the B-24s' procession further into German airspace the Schweinfurt B-17 formation was nearby, and its presence drew some of the Luftwaffe fighters away from the 392nd until the Fortresses turned away towards their target.

A navigational error by the lead B-24 combat wing initially resulted in the wrong attack heading being taken but crews from the 392nd spotted the mistake and were able to guide most of the attacking force back onto the correct track for the Gotha factory.

Miraculously, though partially thanks to assistance from the protecting US fighters, the 392nd only lost one B-24 before bomb release and that was with just minutes to run to the target but six more would fall in quick succession.

The 392nd's first casualty was at 1318hrs when 2nd Lt JV Johnston's B-24 'O-Oboe' exploded during the bomb run. Only two parachutes were seen to appear before the aircraft hit the ground. A moment later 'H-Howe' flown by 2nd Lt TJ Cox was attacked by a reported five Fw 190s. The aircraft banked away from the rest of the formation with its number three engine on fire, but an explosion wrecked the aircraft and it crashed with its bombs still on board. Two aircraft had been destroyed in the three minutes preceding the first of the 392nd's bombs being released at 1321hrs. Next to fall was 2nd Lt JV Barnett's aircraft. Attacked by fighters, its crew was able to release its bombs moments before the aircraft exploded and crashed in the target area. Only three of its ten crew survived. Almost simultaneously 2nd Lt JB Paterson's 'U-Uncle' exploded having released its bombs. Three parachutes were seen to open before the B-24 and its bombs fell in the target area.

The Liberator formation turned for home, but the fighter attacks continued for about another hour. B-24 'L-Love' suffered an engine fire after being hit during a fighter attack and began to lose altitude but its pilot, 1st Lt MT Johns was able to retain enough control to make a successful forced landing. At 1338hrs, 17 minutes after bomb release, 2nd Lt Robert White's 'X-X-ray' succumbed to fighter attacks; three of its crew were able to parachute to safety. Soon afterwards 'W-William' flown by 2nd Lt ME Schlossberg was seen to break up in mid-air following a series of attacks but five of its crew survived. The rest of the 392nd's aircraft were able return to airfields in England, but not necessarily their home base as some made emergency landings at the first available airfields. Some aircraft carried casualties. 'K-King' 41-21941 flown by 2nd Lt ET Wittel limped home with two dead air gunners aboard; both Tech Sgt J Polonchan

> **As Allied preparations for what would become the Normandy landings intensified, so did the attacks on aircraft production facilities**

and Staff Sgt Donald Miller having been killed by Luftwaffe gunfire.

Post-raid photographic reconnaissance of the Gotha target determined the main aircraft production site – believed to produce almost a third of the Luftwaffe's twin-engined fighters – had been largely destroyed and many other buildings damaged. The results put the 392nd's 72 men killed or missing on February 24, 1944, in context. It was the unit's costliest day of the war at that point, but the Gotha factory would never regain its previous full production capacity. That night the RAF followed-up the USAAF attack on Schweinfurt but subsequent analysis deemed little damage was done to aircraft production.

The last daytime attacks of Big Week took place on February 25 when the USAAF's 1st Bombardment Group launched a two-pronged 268 B-17 attack against snow covered Augsburg (218 aircraft) and Stuttgart (50 aircraft). The RAF attacked

LEFT: On February 25/26, 1944, Bomber Command sent almost 600 aircraft to attack the industrial capabilities of Augsburg. Good visibility led to accurate bombing and about 60% of the city's manufacturing capability was destroyed. Augsburg was the last location attacked during Operation Argument.
FRED ROMERO CC BY 2.0

ABOVE: The tragic consequences of the February 22, 1944, USAAF attack on Nijmegen were deliberately 'hushed up' for decades after the war. NIJMEGEN REGION ARCHIVE

Augsburg the same night and aided by unseasonably excellent visibility and assisted by the extra illumination from the snow-covered ground, the bombers destroyed most of the city centre. Frozen rivers and smashed water mains severely hampered the efforts of Augsburg's fire service enabling uncontrolled infernos to spread and consume much of the surrounding industrial area during the early hours of February 26. The 'Argument' was over, now the analysis would begin.

Analysis

Was Big Week a success? In terms of disabling Nazi aircraft production, no. Despite significant damage to several aircraft factories, aircraft production returned to something approaching normal at most sites and was even increased at others. By slowing the production of other types in favour of fighters, the number of fighters delivered would actually increase.

RIGHT: Air Chief Marshal Sir Arthur Harris, seen here at his headquarters desk in April 1944, saw Operation Argument as an unnecessary diversion away from his preferred area bombing policy, but orders from his superior forced him to comply. IWM

Was it a success it terms of attrition? Arguably, yes.

USAAF 8th Air Force bombers flew more than 3,000 missions from the UK while their 15th Air Force compatriots flew approximately 500 from its Italian airfields in the five-day period. The 8th AF lost 137 bombers with 20 more being scrapped when considered beyond repair.

The 15th AF lost 90 bombers and RAF Bomber Command 131. Those numbers are undoubtedly high, but as the number of aircraft taking part in operations which much greater than usual, the percentage losses were lower than average and far smaller than the devastating losses suffered attacking Regensburg and Schweinfurt the previous year. By comparison, the Luftwaffe lost 262 fighter aircraft with approximately 250 aircrew killed or injured, including more than 100 pilots with significant combat experience dead.

The Allies could replace their men and machines fast enough to maintain their front-line fighting force but with Germany fighting increasingly large daily battles on two fronts it was unable the replace its losses and, even more importantly, its pilots' experience levels inevitably declined.

Big Week wasn't the death knell the Allies hoped it would be, but it was another blow that contributed to the Nazi forces' eventual collapse. ∎

NUREMBERG NIGHTMARE

There was never a good time to be flying with Bomber Command, but the night of March 30-31, 1944, was unquestionably the costliest in the RAF's entire history. For almost two years previously, Air Vice-Marshal Arthur Harris, Bomber Command's commander-in-chief, had had a virtually free hand in choosing targets. His aim was to destroy Nazi Germany's will and ability to fight by inflicting major damage upon German cities by mass area bombing raids. Harris was instrumental in evolving Bomber Command from an initially ineffective force into the mighty sledgehammer it became as the war progressed.

Although Harris' preferred area bombing tactic was controversial by some detractors, it had scored some big successes, notably from 1943 with the battles of the Ruhr in the spring and early summer, followed by the devastating Hamburg raids in late July. Nevertheless, Harris' hope of defeating Germany by bombing alone, without the need for a land invasion, was still little more than a dream.

The success of the early '1,000 bomber raids' led Harris to focus on the toughest target of all, the German capital, Berlin. The subsequent 'Battle of Berlin,' starting in the autumn of 1943 and continuing through the following winter, was less successful. Ten raids against the colloquial 'big city' resulted in an astonishing 625 aircraft and over 4,000 aircrew lost.

As part of the preparations for the Normandy invasion, from April 1, 1944, Bomber Command was to be diverted from the area bombing of cities to hitting pre-invasion targets, so the night of March 30 was a 'last chance' for Harris to strike a big blow against a target of his choice before the decision was taken away from him.

Target Nuremberg

Weather conditions were always a crucial aspect of raid planning, but wartime conditions made it difficult to forecast what the weather would be like deep into Germany; little information was available from the continent and a further complication was the half-moon present that night. The bright moonlight would assist the night-fighter force until the moon set in the early hours of the next morning.

There were also two important weather features to consider for the night ahead.

A low air-pressure area over Norway was causing Cumulus cloud to flow over the North Sea and any aircraft flying north of a line from the Humber Estuary to northern Holland would face the risk of icing.

Secondly, a complex cold front extended east from Ireland, through France, southern Germany, and the Balkans before swinging north to its source: a deep depression centred in Russia. This front was moving slowly south, and expectations were that its leading edge would probably contain low cloud that

ABOVE:
Bomber Command fought countless battles in the night skies over Germany, but none were costlier than Nuremberg raid on the night of March 30/31, 1944.
CROWN COPYRIGHT

RIGHT:
Sqn Ldr Paul Jousse – left, 51 Squadron's Rhodesian senior navigator – helps Fg Off Harry Bowling with his flight plan for what was his first, and only, operation. He was killed just hours later. 51 SQUADRON RECORDS

The nightmare story of how Royal Air Force Bomber Command lost more men in a single night than Fighter Command had during the entire Battle of Britain. **WORDS:** TOM ALLETT

bombers to fighter attacks in the bright moonlight. The possibility of high cloud forming on the back of the cold front – which might help to conceal the bomber force – favoured a target in the south.

Another factor favouring a long-range attack was the changing seasons. Winter was changing to spring and the nights would soon be shortening, thereby preventing deep penetration attacks into Germany. Everything pointed towards this being the last opportunity to strike deep into the heart of Germany before the invasion.

In line with Operation Pointblank, the Western Allies' doctrine to smash aircraft and ball-bearing production facilities, the Air Ministry had given Harris a list of priority targets. At the end of March 1944 these were Schweinfurt, Leipzig, Brunswick, Regensburg, Gotha, and Augsburg. Harris didn't agree with these priorities but was forced to consider them. Brunswick, Leipzig, and Gotha were all too far north, Augsburg too far south. Schweinfurt and Regensburg were in the general area Harris was considering, but he turned away from them and consulted the list of area targets: those industrial cities that had not yet been seriously damaged. One name immediately became obvious – Nuremburg. He was handed the Nuremberg file. It recorded that the city contained several important industrial concerns believed to be making tanks, armoured cars, diesel engines, electrical goods and much more. It had not been heavily bombed for seven months and no serious damage was inflicted. There was also the added attraction of its strong association with the Nazi party. Harris made his decision: tonight, there would be a 'maximum effort' against Nuremberg.

Planning

The basic plan required the bombers to take off late in the evening, follow the line of possible high cloud and use the expected tailwind to attempt a swift passage into Germany. Bomb aiming would be by the light of the moon and the return journey could be made in the dark after the moon had set. Harris was gambling on the weather conditions and the reaction time of the German defences, but every raid was a gamble to some extent. If the forecast high cloud did not materialise in the next 12

would cover a potential target. Its trailing edge would possibly contain high layered cloud combined with a strong westerly wind. Elsewhere, there would be very little cloud over Germany.

Combined, this limited Harris' options. northern Germany could not be considered because of the heavy cloud coming down over the North Sea and the large clear sky area inland that would expose the

NUREMBERG

LEFT: "Gentlemen, your target for tonight is..." - Sqn Ldr Peter Hill briefs his crews at RAF Snaith on the afternoon of March 30. Within hours, he and 34 others in the room would be dead.
51 SQUADRON RECORDS

hours, then the operation could be cancelled – as they often were.

Harris then left his headquarters, and his staff were left to plan the route and exact timings. The attack would commence at 0110hrs British Double Summer Time (Zero Hour) and the aiming point for the bomb aimers would be the railway marshalling yards in the centre of Nuremberg.

There were two alternative routes. A direct approach would mean minimum flying time over enemy territory, thereby shortening the danger period. The shorter flying time would increase the potential bomb load, but also give the Germans a better chance of plotting the course and intercepting the bombers.

The alternative was an indirect approach which involved changing course on several smaller legs which kept the Germans guessing about the target but lost the advantages of the direct route.

The route eventually chosen required the bomber stream to form up over the North Sea with every aircraft being given a precise time and height to be there.

The idea was to conceal the identity of the target for as long as possible. The route tracked down into Belgium and then headed east to avoid the notorious Ruhr and Frankfurt anti-aircraft flak defences.

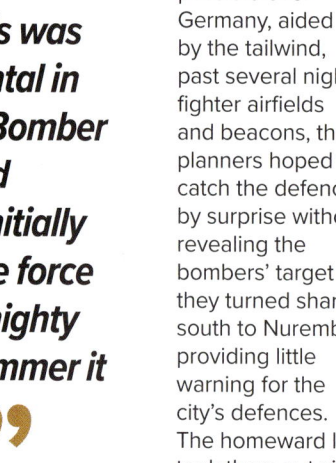

> **Harris was instrumental in evolving Bomber Command from an initially ineffective force into the mighty sledgehammer it became**

Flying as fast as possible over Germany, aided by the tailwind, past several night-fighter airfields and beacons, the planners hoped to catch the defences by surprise without revealing the bombers' target until they turned sharp south to Nuremberg, providing little warning for the city's defences.

The homeward leg took them out via a southerly route, clear of the major flak areas and night-fighter airfields, but it would be a long five-hour slog home into the headwind.

When presented to the Group commanders, objections were raised. AVM Don Bennett, the Commander of 8 Group – the Pathfinders – with his experienced navigators preferred an indirect route, but most of the other groups wanted to stick with the straight in route. For No's 1 and 5 Groups this was because it meant their Lancasters could carry more bombs, while 6 Group favoured it because it meant their Halifaxes were at risk for less time.

Several diversionary, or 'spoof' attacks were planned. Some 50 old Halifaxes would cross the North Sea to simulate a much larger force at about the same time, but turn back before the coast, and Mosquito aircraft would attack Aachen, Cologne, and Kassel, dropping Target Indicator flares as if they were the start of major raids on these towns.

There would also be maximum support from Mosquito intruder squadrons which would patrol the German night-fighter airfields in an attempt to prevent them taking off. They would be assisted by Serrate-equipped Mosquito units which could home in on the German night-fighters' radar emissions. In total, 162 support aircraft were provided, none of which would bomb Nuremberg.

When one of the Serrate Mosquito pilots saw the proposed route, he was concerned that it passed very close to a German visual beacon that he knew to be an assembly point for night-fighters. His concerns were passed to Bomber Command HQ, but the route would not be changed.

BELOW: Sqn Ldr Peter Hill lands Halifax LV777/MH-F after its pre-op air test. He and his crew were killed during the Nuremberg Raid.
51 SQUADRON RECORDS

ABOVE:
The announcement of the night's target was always a moment of high tension in any bomber briefing…
51 SQUADRON RECORDS

When he asked to be allowed to go out to the beacon ahead of the bombers this was also refused.

The individual squadrons had to nominate their crews for the raid. The flight commanders knew this was not one for the new boys and several of the older, more experienced crews, had their leave cancelled or were brought back from local leave. Even so, several of the brand-new arrivals had to be nominated to fly that night.

At 1525hrs a Mosquito of the Met Flight landed at RAF Wyton having flown a wide circuit over Germany to assess the weather without giving the game away.

The information was immediately passed to Bomber Command HQ and the Met forecaster provided an updated brief. The high cloud over the south of Germany was expected to break up before nightfall and there were large amounts of cloud around Nuremberg. This was passed to Harris. His staff expected the raid to be cancelled and were surprised when it was not.

During the pre-departure briefings the bomber crews were informed there would be high cloud on the route out but clear over Nuremberg. They were also told many fighter squadrons had been moved to the coast and that the Americans had inflicted considerable damage to the German night-fighter force during daylight raids.

Many of the more experienced crews came out of briefing with a deep foreboding, even though they knew there was nothing they could do about it. The new crews were not so concerned, they had faith in the Met and Ops briefs, but they were in the minority.

Airborne

Of the 782 Lancasters and Halifaxes detailed to attack Nuremberg, the first airborne was a Lancaster from 103 Squadron at Elsham Wolds at 2116hrs. It took off earlier than the rest because the aircraft had had two new engines and a new mid-upper turret fitted and there had been no time for a dedicated air test. The test was carried out after take-off and, if satisfactory, the aircraft was to continue to Nuremberg.

At East Kirkby, the first departure was 630 Squadron's ME650 flown by P/O Watts: airborne at 2146hrs. The following 33 aircraft took off at about one-minute intervals until the last one – another 630 Squadron aircraft, JB288, flown by F/O ▶

LEFT:
Smiles all round: a crew from 51 – seemingly in good spirits – draw their equipment from the parachute store at Snaith before heading to their aircraft.
ALAMY STOCK PHOTO

NUREMBERG

Johnson from Nassau in the Bahamas – at 2227hrs. Johnson and his crew climbed into the night sky and disappeared from sight, never to be seen again. Their fate is unknown, and they remain 'missing' to this day.

All through eastern England the night was filled with the thundering roar of over 3,000 engines straining to haul the heavily laden bombers into the air.

There were three departure incidents. At Coningsby, a Lancaster suffered a flap failure during the take-off run and would not climb. It struck a marker post just beyond the runway which ripped open a fuel tank and damaged the tailplane, but the aircraft staggered into the air and landed after all the others had gone.

At Skellingthorpe another Lancaster had a tyre burst during take-off. It came off the runway and broke up, but again there were no injuries. At Breighton, a Halifax lost an escape hatch during its take-off run. Again, no harm was done, but the aircraft was out of the raid leaving 779 bombers 'safely' on their way.

The aircraft circled, gaining height, and then set off on course to the rendezvous as planned.

At this point, the weather was good and navigation easy by using the 'Gee' navigational device fitted to all aircraft.

Some aircraft had another navigation aid: H2S, a ground mapping radar mounted under the aircraft that in favourable conditions could pick up large features such as towns, coastlines, and rivers. However, what the RAF did not know was that the H2S transmissions could be detected by the Germans at great distances.

Many of the bombers, 52 in all, turned back due to various technical problems but 727 aircraft crossed the enemy coast on time and on track: approximately 420 miles

> **The night of March 30 was a 'last chance' for Harris to strike a big blow against a target of his choice before the decision was taken away from him**

ABOVE: Ground staff give the crew of LW544/MH-Q a good luck wave as it takes off for a pre-op air test from Snaith in early 1944. It, and its crew, never returned from Nuremberg. 51 SQUADRON RECORDS

BELOW: All through eastern England the air was filled with the thundering roar of over 3,000 engines straining to haul the heavily laden bombers. KEY COLLECTION

and 103 minutes flying time from Nuremberg.

On reaching their turning point south of Brussels many crews were alarmed to find there was no sign of the forecast high cloud. The moon was bright and the visibility clear; and they knew their planned track - a straight line stretching 270 miles - would take them right next to two night-fighter beacons.

Another problem was the wind. The direction and strength had changed from that briefed and the initially compact bomber stream was beginning to disperse, and some crews started to drift off track.

Another unexpected weather phenomenon encountered was contrails. These were normally only found above 25,000ft but this time, through some quirk of the atmosphere, they started to form behind every bomber giving away precisely the aircraft's position and heading. The tight discipline of following the briefed route and height now began to slip as survival instincts told the experienced crews to leave the bomber stream which was becoming an extremely dangerous place to be.

Defences

The German defence staff had concluded that any bomber raid that evening was likely to be somewhere

ABOVE:
The perils of night bombing and the robust construction of the Halifax are evident in this view of LW642/MH-L following a mid-air collision during a raid on Frankfurt on December 20, 1943. Soon repaired, it was flown by Flt Lt Pawell's crew on the Nuremburg raid – after landing safely in England, they reported a quiet trip!
51 SQUADRON RECORDS

in the south of the country but, because of the weather and moon, would probably be a short-range raid, possibly to the Ruhr. The message was passed down to the fighter squadrons to be on standby.

The aircraft taking off from England were quickly picked up by the German monitoring service: initially the force of Halifaxes heading across the North Sea and, shortly afterwards, the force heading southeast. The German commanders had to decide which was the main force and which the diversion. They guessed correctly, and immediately ordered their night-fighters to take off and orbit the radio beacon 'Ida' just south of the Ruhr.

Luftwaffe fighters were scrambled all over Germany. More than 200 were gathering at either the 'Ida' or 'Otto' beacons awaiting their opportunity to ambush the now rapidly converging bombers. Both Luftwaffe and RAF crews found themselves in action earlier than they had anticipated. Unteroffizier Erich Handke of night-fighter squadron III/NJG 1 later recorded: "We were flying from Laon and had been told by the running commentary that the bombers were about five minutes away. I hadn't even switched on the SN-2 [radar] set when the gunner poked me in the back and pointed; there he is up there, the first one.

"As we came round, we saw another straight away about 200 metres directly above. I switched on my SN-2, but we had dropped 2,000 metres behind in the turn and had lost them. When the set warmed up, I saw three targets on it at once. I headed for the nearest and picked it up visually at 600 metres. Weather was marvellous – clear sky, half-moon, little cloud, and no mist – it was simply ideal, almost too bright. It was a Lancaster flying nicely on a steady course so that when we were comfortably positioned underneath and from about 50 metres, we opened fire with the upward firing cannon at one wing which immediately caught fire. We followed the Lancaster for five minutes until it crashed below with a tremendous explosion."

Between the German border and the Rhine, ten Lancasters and two Halifaxes were shot down. One of the Lancasters was downed by 'friendly fire' from a Halifax crew who thought it was a fighter homing in on them. The Lancaster's rear gunner survived to tell the tale; and one of the Halifaxes was shot down by the Coblenz flak.

Because of the unexpected change of wind direction, many of the bombers drifted north and directly over the Ida beacon, straight into the holding fighters.

Another aid to the night-fighters was the Luftwaffe use of flares to light up the night sky and these highlighted the bombers' locations. A special squadron of Junkers Ju88s were trained to fly high above the bomber stream and, when they saw aircraft, they released flares which would bring the fighters in. That night, the conditions were ideal for this tactic. The majority of the bombers shot down – believed to total 61 – were lost during this long (20 minute) straight segment of the route as other bomber crews – in such good visibility – watched with horror as a seemingly endless number ▶

RIGHT:
The casualties, 545 aircrew dead plus 159 others taken as prisoners of war were Bomber Command's highest during a single night for the entire war. This is the shattered remains of 51 Squadron Halifax LW544/HW-Q.
51 SQUADRON RECORDS

NUREMBERG

of flaming wrecks fell from the sky. Those that got through had just survived the worst single hour in Bomber Command's entire war.

Two German fighter pilots each downed four bombers during the Nuremberg raid but the highest number of kills that night was seven, achieved by Oberleutnant Martin Becker. In 30 minutes between the Rhine and the end of the 'long leg' he destroyed three Lancasters and three Halifaxes, before shooting down another Halifax as he returned to base. Despite the carnage, the survivors were closing in on Nuremberg, now some 75 miles and 20 minutes flying time away. The surviving crews – around 650 of them – were now ready to turn south towards their target. Unbeknown to them, they faced a complex situation. Inaccurate wind data was causing some crews to drift off course and the thick cloud which had been expected to clear the target area still lingered over most of the city. Combined with a stronger than expected crosswind, it made the target marking task much more difficult for the leading Pathfinder aircraft. The once single stream of bombers was now effectively split in two, the majority of which had strayed off course and were now heading in the wrong direction. These aircraft were now facing most of the night-fighter attacks. The thick cloud and stronger than predicted winds ruined the accuracy of the attack, and most bombs were released in the vicinity of a nearby medium sized town called Lauf around 10-12 miles northeast of Nuremberg. None of the more than 600 returning bombers brought back photographic evidence of hitting the intended target although over 500 of them brough back images of solid cloud cover, taken at the moment of bomb release. Ironically, some aircraft mistakenly bombed Schweinfurt - the city at the top of the list of targets that Harris had been urged to attack, only to be ignored in favour of Nuremberg.

Casualties

Looking back from a historic perspective, there are two names that stand out from the night's extensive list of casualties suffered on the run-in to Nuremberg. One of the kills achieved by long-established Luftwaffe 'Ace' Oberleutnant Martin Becker that night was Lancaster ND390 / OF-S of 97 Squadron. All seven of its crew were killed, including its rear-gunner, Flt Lt Richard Trevor-Roper DFC, DFM, who had been Guy Gibson's rear-gunner on the Dams Raid in May 1943.

Another nearby crash site was that of the 433 Squadron RCAF Halifax III, HX272 / BM-N. The aircraft was nicknamed *Nielson's Nuthouse* after its pilot, P/O Nielson, and its flight engineer was Flight Sergeant Christopher Panton, the brother of Fred and Harold Panton, founders of the Lincolnshire Aviation Heritage Centre at East Kirkby, which is home to Avro Lancaster *Just Jane* today.

Wherever they had bombed, the surviving crews turned west to start the long slog home. Although still pursued by fighters, the threat against them was now significantly reduced as the bombers, free of their bombs, were faster and more manoeuvrable and the 'hunters' were now low on fuel. The moon finally set at 0148hrs making the bombers more difficult to see without radar assistance but up to nine more bombers were lost on the long flight home - some brought down by flak, while two bombers crashed after a mid-air collision.

While the weather remained satisfactory at many of the RAF airfields some were affected by early morning mist as the bombers approached home. Several crews, their aircraft either damaged or low on fuel, started diverting to alternate locations such as the emergency airfields at Woodbridge and Manston. Not all made it down safely, with 14 aircraft crashing or being written-off on landing, bringing the total number of aircraft lost that night to 109.

One of these was a Halifax piloted by P/O Cyril Barton.

Barton's aircraft had been attacked on the 'long leg' and sustained terrible damage, all turrets were out of action, one engine had failed, the radio and intercom were damaged, and two fuel tanks were leaking.

LEFT: 51 Squadron debrief – the strain of the previous eight hours is evident on the faces of Plt Off Mike O'Loughlin's crew – one of only three to return to RAF Snaith that fateful night. In the centre is bomb aimer Flt Sgt Ian Craib, on his right, O'Loughlin and on his left at the head of the table is navigator Sgt McCoss. 51 SQUADRON RECORDS

ABOVE: Nuremberg was attacked on more than 20 occasions, but it wasn't until 1945 that major damage was inflicted. USAF

Through a misunderstanding in the chaos his navigator, bomb aimer, and wireless operator had abandoned the aircraft. Barton would have been quite justified in dumping his load of incendiaries and turning for home, but instead he continued. He probably bombed Schweinfurt due to his navigational problems and then faced the long return flight on three engines with no navigator or wireless operator to get a radio fix. He had no problems over occupied territory but then appears to have flown up the North Sea paralleling, but just out of sight of, the coast. He made landfall 200 miles further north than he expected over County Durham but then ran out of fuel. The aircraft crash-landed at Ryhope Colliery. His remaining three crew members survived the impact, but Barton was killed. He was later posthumously awarded the Victoria Cross for his outstanding actions; it was the only VC awarded to a Halifax crew member.

There was, however, another fatality resulting from the crash. Colliery pit winder, George Heads (61), had the misfortune to be in the wrong place at the wrong time. When Barton's Halifax broke-up, part of a wing section landed in the gangway leading to the pit. George Heads was found underneath it. Mr Heads was on his way to work when he heard the air-raid sirens sound the all-clear. Knowing his wife was a little hard of hearing he told a colleague he was returning home to tell her it was safe. As he walked home, he was struck by the wing. Mr Heads is believed to be the only British civilian fatality associated with the Nuremberg raid of March 30/31, 1944.

The last aircraft to land was a Lancaster from RAF Waterbeach. It had been diverted from one airfield to another several times due to fog before its pilot eventually put the aircraft down in a field at 0725hrs with no injuries. The Nuremberg raid was over.

Analysis

To keep things in proportion, despite all the described carnage, over 500 aircraft had taken off, dropped their bombs deep in southern Germany and returned to England without encountering a fighter or being hit by Flak. Nevertheless, many returning crews had witnessed numerous aerial battles along their route and some had said the moonlight was so bright and the visibility so clear they were able to read the individual identification letters on the fuselages of bombers flying nearby. Some RAF staff officers initially refused to believe the number of aircraft reportedly lost but detailed analysis over the next 24 hours proved 109 aircraft lost either shot down or crashed, 545 aircrew killed, and 159 taken prisoner. The RAF had lost more aircrew in a single night than it had during the entire Battle of Britain four years earlier.

What was achieved? There was minimal damage in Nuremberg - one factory severely damaged and three others slightly so. The accidental bombing of Schweinfurt hardly affected the ball-bearing production and there were ten unconfirmed claims of German aircraft destroyed.

Several tactical changes took place in the bombing campaign after the Nuremberg raid. Control over Bomber Command was transferred to the Supreme Allied Expeditionary Force so the heavy bombers could be fully harnessed for preparations for the invasion of Europe. The single bomber stream was never used again. Instead, several smaller raids would be mounted and the Master Bomber concept – having a dedicated crew watching the bombing accuracy and issuing any necessary corrections – was introduced.

Even though this particular raid could be seen as nothing but a failure, on many nights the bombing campaign was a great success and the sacrifice made by those young airmen undoubtedly shortened the war by many years and saved countless thousands of Allied lives. For several years, the bomber offensive was the only way of taking the fight to the enemy's homeland and it tied up millions of enemy personnel and valuable resources the Nazis could otherwise have used elsewhere. The RAF crews did not die in vain. ■

D-DAY

THE MOST CRITICAL 24 HOURS

The D-Day invasion of Normandy was arguably the most crucial day of the war on the western front. Allied air power had played a major role in preparing the way for the amphibious assault upon the Normandy beaches, but how effective was it on the day of the invasion? **WORDS:** KEN DELVE

During the evening of June 5, 1944 air bases throughout England became a hive of activity as aircraft were prepared for the first missions of D-Day. Crews filed into hushed briefing rooms. At Bungay in Suffolk, the crews of the 446th Bomb Group learnt they were to be the first US 8th Air Force bombers into the attack. "You are to strike the beach defences at Pointe de la Percée, dropping your bombs not later than two minutes before Zero Hour [0630hrs]. Landing craft and troops will be 400yds to one mile offshore as we attack, and naval ships will be shelling our targets onshore."

At last, the long-awaited invasion had arrived, and it brought a widespread sense of satisfaction. The Operational Record Book (ORB) for the RAF's 402 Squadron states: "This morning at 4am when the boys were getting ready for their first patrol, the groundcrew were told and they cheered. The uplift in morale was good to see. All pilots and groundcrew realised the big day had arrived and they took a new lease of life and went about their work with renewed keenness."

It was the same story at most bases. All knew that it would be the prelude to days of intense effort and that there would be losses – but everyone knew that the war was a step nearer to ending.

Although precise figures of Allied aircraft available vary from source to source, it is certain that they exceeded 10,000 and the potential bomb lift was greater than any previously available.

Preparing the assault area

Allied air power had spent weeks on its pre-invasion bombing strategy and great reliance was now placed on the medium and heavy bombers being used in a tactical bombing role during the assault phase.

Among the first offensive operations taking place in the early hours of June 6 was a variety of 'nuisance' raids by Mosquitos and B-25 Mitchells. Mosquito missions included 48 aircraft to various airfields, gun positions, searchlight sites, bridges, and any trains they happened to find. A further 98 Mosquitos patrolled the area of Rennes-Le Mans-Lisieux between 2200 and 0556hrs with instructions to attack road and rail junctions.

BELOW: Boston IV BZ312 'OA-E' of 342 (French) Squadron returns to Hartford Bridge (now Blackbushe Airport) after completing its D-Day tasks. AUTHOR'S COLLECTION

LEFT:
A 9th Air Force Marauder over the landing beaches. Despite the odd puff of smoke this rather peaceful-looking image belies the intensity of the land battle taking place below.
US NATIONAL ARCHIVES

One of the primary bombing operations for the morning was a series of attacks against the major coastal gun sites. RAF Bomber Command dispatched 1,335 aircraft to attack ten of the gun batteries, hoping to drive the gun crews into their shelters, thereby removing them from the fight. Naval bombardment would then take up the attack against the guns as soon as it was light enough to allow accurate spotting.

The first bombs fell on Crisbecq battery just before midnight on June 5 as two Mosquito marker aircraft led 92 Lancasters of No.1 Group into the attack. Although the target was covered by cloud, the bombers were able to distinguish the glow from the target markers and released 533 tons of bombs. A few minutes later and the second Lancaster force from No.1 Group was releasing its load over a cloud-covered Saint-Martin-de-Varreville. Meanwhile a Halifax/Lancaster force from No.6 (RCAF) Group was making its way to the site at Merville, the first bombs going down at 0025hrs.

There was then a gap before the next Bomber Command raid but then a relentless bombardment began. An attack by 100 Halifaxes from 4 Group dropped 525 tons of bombs on Maisy at 0314 hours. Just 17 minutes later the Lancasters of 5 Group began their attack on La Pernelle. As this raid was taking place, so another force of Halifaxes from 6 Group dropped on Houlgate. Next was Longues where 92 Lancasters dropped 537 tons of bombs through complete cloud cover. Within a minute of the bombers leaving this target at 0428, the first bombs were falling on Mont Fleury and, shortly afterwards, Saint Pierre-du-Mont.

The final attack of the series was made by 110 Lancasters against Ouistreham from 0502 to 0515 hours. According to the RAF narrative: "...there was no real opposition from these batteries during the landing phase – Bomber Command had successfully accomplished the first major air task in the assault." While this statement is in general terms accurate, some gun sites did engage Allied shipping, albeit with little result.

The American bombers had the task of suppressing the beach defences as the landing craft were going in on the assault, with strict adherence to a bomb line, whereby the landing craft were not to proceed within 1,000yds of the beaches until a certain time. However, the results were not always appreciated. One US Ranger company commander commented: "The Air Corps might have done better if they ▶

BELOW:
A classic image showing a 98 Squadron Mitchell attacking a German military installation, wreathed in explosions and smoke.
514 SQUADRON RECORDS

D-DAY

LEFT:
Attacking ground targets was a hazardous business; an understandably pensive Typhoon pilot 'admires' the flak hole in the tail of his aircraft. This is Flt Sgt Rush of 245 Squadron.
AUTHOR'S COLLECTION

had landed their planes on the beach and chased the enemy out with bayonets."

The 8th Air Force analysis stated: "The most important and by far the most elaborate D-Day plans concerned the first mission of the day, involving attacks immediately prior to H-Hour against 45 coastal installations between the Orne and the Vire estuaries on the Normandy coast."

The aim of the attacks was the "demoralisation of the enemy frontline defenders and the disruption of communication lines for reserve forces". The British/Canadian landing sector (Gold, Juno, and Sword beaches) was to be covered by the US 8th Air Force's 1st and 3rd Bombardment Divisions, the American Omaha beach area being allocated to the 2nd Bombardment Division and the remaining American sector, Utah, going to the US 9th Air Force. The bombers were working under severe constraints, not least of which was a restriction on hitting certain locations where it was considered that the problems created by bomb craters would outweigh any benefit in the reduction of enemy defensive capability. To this end, most bombs were given instantaneous fuses and only bombs of under 1,000lb were employed.

The beach defences the bombers attacked were often of a type not suitable for medium level bombing. In the case of concrete pillboxes set into sand dunes, where there was very little chance of the bombing doing any physical damage; rather than destroy the pillbox, the intention was to send the defenders to their shelters, allowing the assault troops to land before the enemy had time to recover. Strict timing was paramount.

The first of what was to be four major operations got underway at 0115 hours, with 1,365 bombers despatched by the 8th Air Force. Lt Litwiller was on B-24 *Liberty Run* of the 446th Bomb Group heading for Omaha beach. It was the first aircraft of the US VIII Bomber Command to make an attack this day: "We took off at 0220, climbed to 10,000ft and circled our prescribed forming area. The mission went precisely as planned with the briefed undercast necessitating bombing by H2X radar. As we approached the French coast, the radar navigator called me over to look at his [Pathfinder Force] PFF scope. It indicated the vast armada of the invasion fleet standing just off the coast of Normandy – a thrilling sight even on radar. Bombs were away at 0600."

The 95th Bomb Group, as part of the 3rd Bombardment Division, was tasked against the beaches in the British sector. Its record book states: "Our group of about 40 B-17s in close formation began to ease its way into the narrow corridor for the bomb run. As we reached the beach the lead plane released a smoke bomb, which was the signal for all 40 aircraft to drop their bombs simultaneously.

LEFT:
The rugged Thunderbolt proved an excellent ground attack aircraft, capable of carrying a variety of weapons and taking a fair amount of punishment from ground fire.
US NATIONAL ARCHIVES

LEFT:
Bomber Command 'heavies' flew some of the first 'ops' on June 6, attacking coastal gun batteries. The Lancasters of 83 Squadron were part of the force attacking La Pernelle (not in this photo) in the early hours of the morning, providing aircraft for the Flare Force and the main bombing effort.
AUTHOR'S COLLECTION

Thus, more than 100 tons of bombs exploded in a matter of a few seconds. The explosions caused our aircraft to bounce and vibrate."

War correspondents aboard the ships reported on the attacks: "...the air power that we have seen most forcibly was the final attack by the American 8th Air Force. Immediately before H-Hour they dropped a vast weight of bombs on the beaches. The beaches shook and seemed to rise into the air, and ships well out at sea quivered and shook."

Battering the defenders

After the first waves of heavy and medium bombers cleared their targets, it was the turn of naval gunfire and the fighter-bombers to batter the defenders. The bombardment ships were to be on station at 0500hrs, having moved into position under the cover of a smoke screen laid by RAF Bostons. These ships were capable of laying down a massive amount of firepower, the accuracy and effectiveness of which was down to the aircraft of the Air Spotting Pool (ASP), based at Lee-on-Solent and comprising four Fleet Air Arm Seafire squadrons of No.3 Naval Wing, five RAF squadrons, plus Spitfires operated by US Naval Squadron VCS-7.

Most sorties, certainly in the early phase, consisted of counter-battery work against coastal guns, field artillery and flak positions. Aircraft of the ASP flew more than 400 sorties during the day on 135 shoots. About 50% were considered successful, despite many being aborted due to communication problems.

The first waves of fighter-bombers were given pre-arranged targets to hit at H-Hour. Most were on or just behind the beaches and all based upon the latest air reconnaissance information.

The Contact Parties or Army Tentacles/US Air Support Parties went ashore with the initial waves, the intention being that they could radio for air support from on-call aircraft. With clearance to attack any enemy movement, or suspected enemy movement not displaying recognition markers, the fighter-bombers harassed every road in Normandy.

The 2nd TAF's medium bombers were tasked to harass enemy road and rail movement and to destroy/disrupt movement through road and rail chokepoints. The role of the three B-25 Mitchell squadrons of No.139 Wing at Dunsfold was typical, the general instruction having been expressed in Operational Order No 3: "...to cause the maximum delay to the movement by road and rail, by enemy forces at night, in the area prescribed, any movement is to be attacked whenever seen in the area."

During the early hours of D-Day each squadron had a specific objective. Running towards their target of a road/rail crossing north of Argentan, the 12 Mitchells of 180 Squadron found weather conditions worse than forecast. Nevertheless, eight aircraft managed to identify and bomb the target. Meanwhile, the 12 aircraft of 320 Squadron were having great difficulty in finding their road bridge over the Dives River and ▶

LEFT: Sgt Bob Fairborn, Plt Off Harold Tracey, and Sgt Ray Cowan of 429 Squadron after their D-Day operation.
AUTHOR'S COLLECTION

BELOW LEFT: Bulletin Board of the 391st BG, June 6, 1944. The group was part of an intensive USAAF effort to neutralise the beach defences ahead of the assault wave landings.
AUTHOR'S COLLECTION

BELOW RIGHT: Marauders of the 386th BG at Great Dunmow being given their 'invasion stripes'. The Allies were concerned about friendly fire losses (from ships and aircraft), hence the use of stripes on wings and fuselage, although RAF Bomber Command was an exception to this. AUTHOR'S COLLECTION

D-DAY

ABOVE: A Mustang of 2 Squadron took this view of the landings on the evening of June 6, 1944.
AUTHOR'S COLLECTION

RIGHT: Crews from the 381st BG receive their D-Day briefing.
AUTHOR'S COLLECTION

RIGHT: P-51s played a dual role as part of the air screen but also, once released from their patrol, went hunting ground movements – a hazardous role; this Mustang hit a tree while on a low-level strafe attack.
AIR HISTORICAL BRANCH

almost total cloud cover led to this target being aborted.

The final wing operation was that of 98 Squadron's 11 Mitchells to a road defile south of Thury-Harcourt. In the British sector, 12 squadrons of Typhoons were tasked with attacking strong points, beach defences, batteries, and HQs, at H-Hour. Typically, No.146 Wing was ordered to attack the tank concentration area near Bayeux, claiming four tanks destroyed and five damaged, while No.121 Wing attacked gun batteries overlooking Omaha beach.

An equally important task was to keep the enemy commanders confused, and what better way than attacking HQs and communications sites. At 0745hrs eight bomb-equipped Typhoons attacked an HQ complex at Sainte Croix-Grand-Tonne with reasonable results. Another HQ, at La Meauffe Chateau, was attacked by rocket-equipped Typhoons an hour or so later. Numerous other installations were attacked on an opportunity basis and great confusion was caused. The 'fog of war' suffered by the German commanders was very much a result of Allied air power which led to critical command decisions being delayed or made in error.

On Sword beach the plan worked well and the troops of the 3rd British Division faced little opposition. A few enemy strong points came to life again and could have caused serious problems. At Gold, the Typhoons failed to neutralise the strongpoint on the left flank at Le Hamel, although some damage had been caused. By the time the assault waves hit the beaches, the defences were fully manned, and casualties rose in the face of determined opposition.

It was a mixed story in the American sector. On Utah beach, attacks by Marauders and fighter-bombers had worked well and the assault troops were able to achieve their objectives with little opposition. However, at Omaha it was a different story. 'Bloody Omaha' resulted in 3,000 Americans being killed or wounded and was a salutary indication of what could have happened if the assault phase, and its air campaign, had been less well planned and executed.

Isolating the beachhead

From late morning onwards most fighter-bomber tasking involved armed reconnaissance to search out road and rail movement. Suitable targets were passed to one of the forward air control units which would then allocate attacking aircraft. Roving Typhoons were responsible for one of the most devastating attacks of the day when aircraft from No.123 Wing spotted German armour moving along the roads towards Caen. This was Panzer Lehr Division and despite objections from its commander, Lt Gen Bayerlein, it had been ordered to move by daylight. Such a promising target was too good to waste, and it was attacked by relays of aircraft throughout the daylight hours. During one of the attacks the Typhoons of 183 Squadron were bounced by Bf 109s and had to jettison their bombs. Nevertheless, three aircraft were shot down and all three pilots killed. The Luftwaffe had proved that it was not totally absent.

Total losses to Panzer Lehr amounted to five Mk IV tanks, 84

ABOVE:
Typhoons operated with guns, bombs, and rockets. This 440 Squadron aircraft has a suitably adorned bomb. AUTHOR'S COLLECTION

BELOW:
Coastal Command was also active on D-Day, keeping the German surface and submarine threat at bay. AUTHOR'S COLLECTION

self-propelled guns/armoured personnel carriers, 40 fuel bowsers and 90 other vehicles. Added to this was the psychological trauma to inexperienced soldiers from such an aerial onslaught. However, the low loss rate among tanks confirmed the view that the RP rocket was not the ideal weapon against such targets. It was difficult to aim and required extensive practise. One analysis suggested that it required 308 RPs to eliminate one tank!

The US VIII Bomber Command flew three more missions during the day, all with the task of keeping German reinforcements away from the beachhead areas. A force of 508 bombers, mainly B-24s, attacked towns and villages on main roads to the south and southwest of Caen, to create roadblocks. The afternoon missions involved 71 B-24s going to Caen, and 738 bombers attacking targets in the Laval area. The medium bombers of the 9th Air Force were also tasked against towns and villages that afternoon, 45 Bostons attacking Carentan at 1430hrs, followed by 24 Marauders to Falaise at 1520hrs and, just an hour later, 73 Marauders to Caen, the latter attack losing one aircraft.

Initial plans to attack the major road routes using medium bombers had to be amended. Low cloud meant the only possible air operation likely to be effective was that by low-flying fighter-bombers. Typhoon patrols were ordered to cover every major route, while in bordering areas this same task was to be performed by P-51s and P-47s.

An evening sweep by 48 Typhoons and 15 P-38 Lightnings in the Caen-Argentan-Lisieux-Bayeux areas paid dividends. The aircraft attacked a wide range of targets with bomb, rocket, and cannon, claiming the destruction of 23 armoured vehicles, one signal box, a variety of soft-skinned transport and a number of sections of railway line.

Sgt Edward Donne of 266 Squadron later recalled: "I took off with eight other Typhoons at about 1700hrs on an armed recce looking for tanks in the area SE of Caen. When we were about 25km south of Caen we saw a column of German transport and bombed it. When I dropped my bomb there was an explosion and I went up with it. The engine was still running, and we carried out another attack, but when returning home about five minutes later, I had no other option but to bale out. This was about 1800hrs. I landed in a field 5km west of Caen."

Sgt Donne moved north and tried to elicit help from two French civilians, who refused to get involved. He carried on and at dusk saw some Sherman tanks, the commander of which sent him by motorcycle to the HQ area. Taken by jeep to the beachhead, he left Normandy on a landing craft tank (LCT) the following night.

> **All knew that it would be the prelude to days of intense effort and that there would be losses**

During the late afternoon, P-47s of the 9th Air Force made two accurate attacks on bridges. The majority of the evening effort by the 9th Air Force was against rail targets and coastal defences. Between 2100 and 2113hrs five attacks were made against rail targets in the assault area, ending bombing operations for the day.

Fighter operations

For the fighter squadrons D-Day was hectic but fairly unproductive, the day's events being summarised in the Fighter Command intelligence summary: "No major encounters took place throughout the first day of the launching of the invasion of Normandy. Enemy air activity was negligible. It is estimated that both escorting and protective fighters ▶

D-DAY

over the assault areas and defensive fighters over France did not exceed 50 to 70 [enemy] sorties."

The Allied expectation had been different, the directive issued to the fighter forces stating: "The intention of the British and American fighter forces is to attain and maintain an air situation which will assure freedom of action for our forces without effective interference by the German Air Force."

Lt Col Don Blakeslee, 4th Fighter Group, briefed his pilots at 0300hrs: "I am prepared to lose the whole Group." The American fighter commands provided the bulk of the escort and high cover patrols throughout the day, the low cover patrols being provided by RAF Spitfires. The plan was to provide a screen of fighters around the entire invasion area from 0425hrs. Should enemy aircraft make it through the outer fighter screen then in the actual beach area additional high cover was provided by three squadrons of P-47s with squadrons of Spitfires acting as low 'beach cover'. Shipping cover over the invasion convoys and Normandy anchorages was provided by six P-38 groups.

Lt Col Dix of the 355th Fighter Group recorded: "For the first mission of D-Day, the 355th was divided into two parts, 'A' Group composed of the 354th and 357th Fighter Squadrons, and 'B' Group consisting of the 358th Squadron. The first mission of the 'big day' turned out to be a quiet one as neither division of the group saw any enemy planes. Handicapped by weather and the darkness, the group was soon split up into sections and flights. It was impossible to orientate the outfit definitely over its assigned area. All told, not one member of the Luftwaffe was on hand to offer resistance to the first phase of the invasion."

Pilot Jerry Jarrold from 80 Squadron recalled: "The squadron flew two missions on D-Day. The first involved two flights of four aircraft acting as cover for a convoy over North Foreland, with the first four airborne at 1100 and down at 1340, and the second four, with me as No.2, airborne at 1205 and down at 1355. It was exceptionally bad weather, and we didn't see much of the ships we were supposed to be patrolling and our patrol saw no action."

However, from mid-afternoon onwards the Luftwaffe made a few sorties, usually tip-and-run attacks against either naval targets or troops coming ashore. German records detail no more than 100 offensive missions flown on this day. Most combats took place late in the day, the most successful being that of the 355th Fighter Group which jumped a formation of Ju 87s and rapidly claimed 15 of them. The US VIII Fighter Command recorded over 1,300 sorties for the day.

Maritime operations

Aircraft of Coastal Command continued their anti-submarine patrols in the expectation that the Germans would attempt to attack the flanks of the invasion fleet.

Early on June 6 several U-boats were spotted on the surface to the south west of Brest, heading towards the invasion area. Although the Germans did not have a large surface fleet in this area, the few available destroyers did pose a threat, as did the larger number of fast attack craft such as the 'E' boats.

For most of the squadrons of 16 and 19 Groups it was to be a day of waiting and yet more waiting as the 'great day' passed them by. However, when a force of three enemy destroyers was spotted heading from the Gironde estuary towards the fleet, a strike force of Beaufighters, with Mosquito escort, was soon on the scene. Thirty Beaufighters, 14 RP-equipped aircraft from 404 Squadron and 16 cannon-firers as anti-flak from 248 Squadron, were led into the attack by Wg Cdr Lumsden. One destroyer was damaged and all three

> **Although precise figures of Allied aircraft available vary from source to source, it is certain that they exceeded 10,000**

ABOVE:
A Wethersfield-based A-20 of the US 416th BG. The unit attacked Le Havre on June 6.
AUTHOR'S COLLECTION

BELOW:
The Avro Lancaster may not be the first aircraft type to spring to mind when considering D-Day operations, but large numbers were involved in strikes during the early hours of the big day.
AUTHOR'S COLLECTION

made for the nearest port. A major U-boat movement from the Bay of Biscay ports was reported later in the day and various units were tasked with hunting them down. It was not until the night hours of June 6 that contact was made, the submarines having surfaced in an attempt to make a high-speed dash into the Channel.

During the night, sightings were reported, the aircraft of 53 Squadron proving particularly alert. Only seven of these detections culminated in attacks and two submarines were claimed destroyed (Type VIICs, U-955 and U-970). However, not all anti-shipping strikes were given to Coastal Command. Just after dawn, a force of Whirlwind bombers of 137 Squadron with a Typhoon escort from 609 Squadron, went after a group of four Class M minesweepers off Ambleteuse. All the aircraft made successful attacks against the enemy ships despite heavy flak from the targets themselves and shore installations.

With so many Allied aircraft crossing the Channel, it was inevitable that some would end up ditching. In the early hours of June 6, the High-Speed Launches (HSLs) took up their positions and waited; the ASR aircraft patrols started before dawn. During the day, a total of 60 aircrew were rescued.

RIGHT:
Most of the USAAF's air superiority missions were performed by Mustangs. This P-51, 51380 'A9-A' carries the markings of the 9th Air Force's 363rd Fighter Group.
AUTHOR'S COLLECTION

BELOW:
The USAAF allocated much of its P-47 strength to ground attack roles. The location of this photograph is uncertain but was possibly taken at Mount Farm.
AUTHOR'S COLLECTION

Reaction times were so quick that one Spitfire pilot was picked up within minutes of baling out – the HSL crew watching him float down and getting as close as they could.

Final judgement

Having studied the crucial aerial activity of arguably the most important day in modern history, the Allied commanders reported: "The unsuitable weather nullified the advantage largely enjoyed by the Allies of overwhelming air superiority. This was largely because the heavy day bombers could not operate effectively in such conditions."

Despite the best efforts of Allied intelligence officers to uncover the facts and figures relating to the effectiveness of the air effort, there was much debate regarding its overall contribution to the day's events. Thus, there will always be a problem when trying to determine what percentage of the overall effort was truly effective and what was 'wasted'. Nevertheless, it is certain that the weight of Allied air power played a significant role in both preparing the battle area and in securing the lodgement ashore. ■

THE LEGEND OF Y-29

SURPRISE ATTACK

Operation Bodenplatte, the Luftwaffe's desperate attempt to regain air superiority in western Europe, ended in defeat and included a remarkable 45-minute skirmish over Asch – perhaps the wildest fight for any USAAF Eighth Air Force fighter unit. **WORDS:** THOMAS MCKELVEY CLEAVER

BELOW: The 'Blue Nose Bastards of Bodney': A flight of North American P-51B/D Mustangs of the 352nd Fighter Group escort a formation of Consolidated B-24 Liberators from the 458th Bomb Group across the English Channel, mid-1944.
KEY COLLECTION

During a November 20, 1944, meeting concerning the Luftwaffe's disastrous performance on November 2 when 80 US bombers were shot down at the cost of 90 German fighters, Hitler overruled Jagdwaffe's (fighter force) commander Adolf Galland's plan for a 'Gross schlag' – or Big Hit – stating the enemy was now too strong in the air. Instead, he directed that every available fighter was to be deployed across western Germany to support a coming operation.

Indefensible loses

Unternehmen Bodenplatte – or Operation Baseplate, the Luftwaffe's last-ditch attempt to cripple Allied air power in the Low Countries – was originally scheduled to start with the launch of the Wehrmacht's offensive across the Ardennes on December 16, 1944. However, that required bad weather to prevent Allied fighter-bombers from taking to the skies. And while the Luftwaffe managed to launch some 500 aircraft on December 16, operating in such conditions proved to be beyond the capability of most units. Adding to the Luftwaffe's woes, over the eight days between December 17 and December 27 when weather conditions allowed

operations, the Jagdwaffe lost 644 fighters while another 227 were damaged. To make matters worse, 322 pilots were killed. Consequently, no one expected a large-scale air operation.

With the weather clearing and more of the Allies' fighter-bombers returning to the skies, the German offensive quickly ground to a halt. As a result, and despite running short of fuel due to Allied strikes against petroleum, oil, and lubrication facilities that summer, the Wehrmacht attempted to restart its offensive under Unternehmen Nordwind (Operation Northwind) on December 31, 1944. Bodenplatte was intended to support this.

The plan called for a surprise attack against 17 Allied airfields and Advanced Landing Grounds (ALG) across Belgium, the Netherlands, and France. Given the objective, every Jagdwaffe Geschwader (wing) was to be involved. Messerschmitt Bf 110s and Junker Ju 88s would act as pathfinders for the attacking Messerschmitt Bf 109s and Focke-Wulf FW 190s.

In the meantime, Ultra (British military intelligence) had picked up several Luftwaffe signals instructing bomber units to co-ordinate with fighter units. However, it mistakenly interpreted that the fighters would be directed against Allied bombers instead of supporting an imminent operation.

In fact, secrecy surrounding the operation was so tight that not all German units involved were informed of its timing. To exacerbate the situation, the planners blundered by choosing flight paths that took several of the units over the V2 rocket launch sites around The Hague in the Netherlands, which were protected by an armada of anti-aircraft artillery – or Triple-A – batteries, in addition to those along the Dutch coast. Consequently, a quarter of the attacking units lost aircraft to 'friendly fire'.

Enter the 'Blue Nose Bastards'

Since arriving in mainland Europe from England in late December 1944, the North American P-51 Mustangs ▶

ABOVE: Seen here in the cockpit of his personal mount, *Petie 3rd*, Lt Col John C Meyer was the deputy commander of the 352nd Fighter Group at the time of the Luftwaffe's attack on Y-29. IWM

> **Despite running short of fuel due to Allied strikes against petroleum, oil, and lubrication facilities that summer, the Wehrmacht attempted to restart its offensive**

THE LEGEND OF Y-29

ABOVE: Before moving to mainland Europe in late 1944, the Mustangs of the 487th Fighter Squadron called RAF Bodney in Norfolk home. Seen here awaiting their next sortie earlier that year, the aircraft that is closest – 44-13530/HO-A *Millie* – was the mount of Lt Kenneth F Wittekiend.
THOMAS CLEAVER

of the USAAF's 352nd Fighter Group (FG), nicknamed 'Blue Nose Bastards of Bodney', had provided early morning patrols over the front lines – which had proven fruitful in combating Luftwaffe activities.

At midnight on January 31, 1945, Lt Col John C Meyer was interrupted while planning the first dawn patrol of the year by orders from 'Football' – the name assigned to the Ninth Air Force's headquarters – directing the 352nd to prepare a 'maximum effort' escort mission the next day. This meant there would be no early morning patrol. Meyer immediately informed his squadron commanders – all of whom were disappointed given how much Luftwaffe fighter activity there was over the 'lines'.

The pilots mulled the order, while looking for a way to comply and still launch a patrol. With countless calls to 'Football' to modify the order unsuccessful, a

> **Secrecy surrounding the operation was so tight that not all German units involved were informed of its timing**

frustrated Meyer turned in, with orders to wake him at dawn in case things changed.

As first light broke on January 1, base Y-29 at Asch, Belgium, was covered in thick fog – which would delay operations. At 0800hrs, Meyer called 'Football' again asking for a change in orders. Gen Elwood Quesada put Meyer on the spot – would he personally state the fighters were needed for patrol because of a threat, and take responsibility for anything that happened if the order was changed?

With Meyer's yes, Quesada approved the patrol at 0845hrs. And, with the fog lifting, the pilots assigned to the patrol got to work. Departing Asch, the Mustangs

ABOVE:
Lt Col J C Meyer's personal mount – North American P-51D Mustang 44-15041/HO-M *Petie 3rd* – is pictured on the ground at Y-29 shortly after the Luftwaffe's surprise attack on January 1, 1945. THOMAS CLEAVER

would head southeast to St Vith – the logistical bottleneck for Wehrmacht activity on the front following their failure to take the Belgian cities of Malmedy and Bastogne – before heading back to cover the escort taking off. Using the 487th Fighter Squadron's (FS) radio callsign 'Transport', 'White', 'Yellow' and 'Red' flights with four aeroplanes each would make up the patrol – Meyer would lead as 'Transport White One'.

Finally, at 0915 hours with the fog lifted, Meyer watched eight Republic P-47 Thunderbolts from the 366th FG's 390th FS take-off as he led 12 blue-nosed P-51s to the runway in his usual machine (42-415041/HO *Petie 3rd*). As Meyer accelerated, he saw the ominous black puffs from anti-aircraft artillery (AAA) ahead of him as tracer from countless machine guns started whipping through the sky. When he asked the control tower what was happening, they replied there was nothing. But as he passed the halfway point of the runway, the flak bursts got thicker, as a line of black specks appeared low on the horizon. Seconds later, one of the specks turned into an FW 190 that seemed to be coming directly at him – all Meyer could do was keep accelerating until he could get the Mustang off the deck. As he did, the enemy fighter opened fire, forcing Meyer to duck.

However, he quickly realised he wasn't the target when he saw a Douglas C-47 Skytrain parked next to the runway take hits. When his airspeed indicator hit 100mph, Meyer hauled his aeroplane off the ground and quickly lifted his landing gear as he pulled the trigger. Watching as his rounds hit the FW 190's engine, it swerved toward him before its nose dropped. As it did, Meyer flew over the stricken fighter – missing it by mere inches. Observers saw the FW 190 hit the ground as the Mustang climbed away. It was initially unclear if they had collided until Meyer was seen banking away beyond the rising cloud of black smoke. By then, the fog was a strong haze, making it difficult to identify shapes in the sky.

As the other Mustangs became airborne behind him, Meyer quickly reached 2,000ft and spied two indistinct shapes ahead. Closing, he fleetingly took them ▶

LEFT:
Second Lieutenant William 'Bill' Whisner – seen here with his original mount, North American P-51B 42-106449/HO-W *Princess Elizabeth* in 1944 – became an 'ace in a day' while fighting over his own airfield on January 1, 1945. USAF

THE LEGEND OF Y-29

for P-47s, before realising it was another pair of FW 190s. Closing on the wingman, he opened fire. As he did, he spotted a Bf 109 curve in on his left rear, but it was still out of range.

Although the FW 190 ahead took multiple hits, he couldn't hold fire on it as he was being bounced around by its propwash. Suddenly, its pilot threw the machine into a 'Split-S' from 3,000ft. As Meyer turned hard left, the now in-range '109 behind fired and missed him – an instant later, a blue-nosed P-51 turned onto the Bf 109's tail and opened fire as the enemy pilot turned away.

Looking for the FW 190, Meyer saw it with streamers spewing from the wingtips. It pulled out so low to the ground, it looked as if it hit the trees. Diving after it to finish the fight, his Mustang shuddered as it was battered by anti-aircraft fire – a hole appearing in his machine's wing. Taking another hit, he turned away from the 'friendly fire' as the '190 started climbing… Meyer opened fire. Hit, the enemy pilot turned looking for somewhere to crash land. But on touching down, his wingtip dug in causing his stricken fighter to somersault, break up and explode. Knowing he was too low on ammunition to re-engage, Meyer departed the battle.

Ace in a day

The eight P-47s that took off just before Meyer were the first to run into the fighters of JG 11 as

> **66** As Meyer accelerated, he saw the ominous black puffs from anti-aircraft artillery (AAA) ahead of him as tracer from countless machine guns started whipping through the sky **99**

they approached Y-29. With the Thunderbolt pilots downing two of the fighters as they flashed through their formation, it distracted the enemy pilots at just the right moment.

Meyer's wingman, 1st Lt Alex Sears flying as 'White Two', remembered: "We had just taken off when we were bounced by 40 or 50 Me 109s and FW 190s. One Me 109 came at me head-on and we made several passes at each other, both of us firing. On the third pass I got some strikes on his engine and shot part of the tail section away. He started burning and went down in a lazy spiral and crashed."

Meyer's element leader, 1st Lt Raymond Henry Littge ('White Three') downed a FW 190 as he lifted off, before chasing another that took hits. Littge kept firing at the machine until he was out of ammunition and followed it until the pilot baled out somewhere near Paris.

Littge's wingman, 2nd Lt Alden Peter Rigby ('White Four') shot an FW 190 off his leader's tail pretty much before his wheels had retracted, before turning onto another. He recalled: "I dropped down on his tail and my gunsight went out – so I fired a long burst

BELOW:
North American P-51D Mustang 44-14778/HO-E *The Sheepherder* taxies at Asch in early 1945 in the hands of Capt Alexander F Sears. Both the man and the machine were veterans of what became known as the 'Legend of Y-29'.
THOMAS CLEAVER

until I noticed hits on his wing roots. He started pouring black smoke and lost altitude until he crashed into the trees. I immediately returned to the field and noticed a P-47 in a Lufbery [circle] with a '109. The P-47 fired a short burst, and I noticed a few strikes on the '109. He tightened his turn – as the P-47 mushed, I came in and fired a long burst. He crashed in an open field." Nearly out of ammunition, Rigby circled to land, but ran across another fight between a pair of P-51s and a Bf 109. He continued: "The '109 broke in my direction and I fired the remainder of my ammo at him – scoring at least one hit in the cockpit. The enemy aircraft dived straight into the ground."

On landing, Rigby claimed two FW 190s and two Bf 109s as 'destroyed', a 'possible' shared with an unidentified P-47 and another 'possible' shared with an unidentified P-51. Despite his claims, he would not get full credit for the two Bf 109s for another 55 years.

Maj William 'Bill' Halton's 'Yellow Flight' followed 'White Flight' into the ensuing chaos almost immediately on leaving the ground. Dodging enemy fighters

RIGHT: 'Bill' Whisner was flying P-51D Mustang 44-14237/HO-W *Moonbeam McSwine* on January 1, 1945.
THOMAS CLEAVER

BELOW: Seen here in the cockpit of his regular Mustang 44-72216/HO-M *Miss Helen*, Capt Raymond H Littge scored two 'kills' flying the same machine on January 1, 1945. Note the missing panel below the port exhaust, suggesting this image was either taken as a keepsake or a publicity shot.
USAF

on take-off, element leader 1st Lt Sanford Moats ('Yellow 3') quickly shot down four FW 190s, while his wingman 2nd Lt Henry Stewart ('Yellow 2') downed three '109s. Similarly, Halton and his wingman, 2nd Lt Dean Huston ('Yellow 4') each claimed an FW 190.

By the time Capt Bill Whisner's 'Red Flight' got airborne, the sky was filled with enemy aircraft. Scoring his first while climbing from take-off, he later reported: "I ran into about 30 FW 190s at 1,500ft. I picked one out and pressed the trigger. Nothing happened. I reached down and turned on my gun switch and gave a couple of good bursts."

As Whisner saw number one hit the ground and explode, he felt his own machine shudder. "A '190 was about 50 yards behind me, firing away," he recalled. "As I was turning with him, another P-51 attacked him, and he broke off his attack. I then saw that I had several 20mm holes in each wing

> **When his airspeed indicator hit 100mph, Meyer hauled his aeroplane off the ground and quickly lifted his landing gear as he pulled the trigger**

and another round had hit my oil tank. My left aileron was also out, and I was losing oil – but my temperature and pressure were steady."

Despite the damage, Whisner was aggressively turning his Mustang toward the ensuing dogfight and quickly caught another FW 190. He remarked: "After I hit him with several bursts, the pilot tried to jump. Just as his canopy came off, I fired again and the '190 rolled over, crashed and exploded." He then came across a flight of Bf 109s and engaged one: "We fought for five or ten minutes, and I finally managed to get behind him. I hit him good, and he went down. At this time, I saw some 15 to 20 fires on the ground – all from crashed airplanes."

As Whisner turned his damaged aeroplane back towards the airfield, it was still under attack.

THE LEGEND OF Y-29

He remembered: "I saw a '109 strafe the northeastern [end] of the strip. I started after him, and he turned into me. We made two head-on passes and on the second I hit him in the nose and wings. He crashed and burned. I chased several more 'bandits', but they evaded me in the clouds. By now my windshield was covered with oil – so I headed back to the strip and landed."

Whisner, already an 11-victory ace, had just become an 'ace in a day' fighting over his own airfield!

Numbers game

At the time of the attack, JG 11 lacked both men and aeroplanes – its I Staffel (I./JG 11) had just 16 FW 190s on strength and six pilots. The lack of numbers was made up by III./JG 11, which had more pilots than aircraft. Despite its efforts, the Jagdgeschwader could only muster 41 FW 190s – four from the Stab (staff) flight, six from I/JG 11 and 31 from III/JG 11, plus 20 Bf 109s from II/JG 11 for the attack. The plan called for the more heavily armed FW 190s to strafe ground targets, while the Bf 109s provided top cover. To make matters worse, four fighters were quickly lost to AAA while crossing the lines. And with their flight path taking them directly over the Allied ALG at Ophoven (Y-32) – just to the northeast of Asch and home to the Supermarine Spitfire XIVs of No.125 Wing RAF – 30 FW 190s and Bf 109s attacked the field thinking it was Y-29.

The 45-minute battle over Asch went into the record books as 'The Legend of Y-29' – it was the wildest fight any Eighth Air Force fighter unit ever engaged in. On landing, the pilots of the 487th were credited with 24 'destroyed' for the loss of no P-51s – although two were damaged during the skirmish and one on the ground.

With many of its surviving aircraft limping home, JG 11 reported the loss of 28 FW 190s and Bf 109s. Four pilots made it back to German territory, four were captured and another 20 were killed – JG 11's Kommodore ObstIt Günther Specht and III/JG 11 Gruppenkommandeur Hptm Horst-Günther von Fassong were among the latter.

The 487th Fighter Squadron's performance was so impressive it was awarded a Distinguished Unit Citation, while Distinguished Service Crosses were bestowed on John Meyer (his third), Bill Whisner (his second) and Sanford Moats for their efforts. Similarly, Maj William Halton, Capt Henry Stewart, and Lts Raymond Littge and Alden Rigby were each awarded the Silver Star. However, for Meyer, the action over Asch

BELOW: A flight of Mustangs equipped with long-range drop tanks from the 352nd Fighter Group taxi for a mission at Asch in March 1945. USAF

was his last – he was injured in a jeep accident a week later and hospitalised for the rest of the war.

He later wrote: "For the first time in my experience in the European air war, American fighters had neither the advantage of superior tactical position, numbers or equipment.

"For the first time, there was no measurement involved in the final determination other than the relative skill and initiative of the pilots. It was no time for leadership or organisation. It was man against man."

Missed opportunity?

Of the 34 Luftwaffe Jagdgruppe's assigned targets, only 11 hit theirs on time without alerting the enemy. But with a total of some 900 fighters participating in the opening action of Bodenplatte, the Jagdwaffe claimed 400 Allied aircraft 'destroyed' on the ground, 79 'destroyed' in the air and another 100 'damaged'.

However, actual Allied losses were said to be just 290 aircraft 'destroyed' and 180 damaged.

It came at a cost – the Jagdwaffe noted 143 pilots were killed or missing, 70 were captured and another 21 wounded. Among the losses were two Geschwaderkommodoren, six Gruppenkommandeuren and 14 Staffelkapitäen.

While Allied aircraft destroyed on the ground were replaced within a week, the Germans found it impossible to replace lost pilots. Obstl Johannes Kogler, Kommodore of JG 6, who survived being shot down, confessed to his American interrogators: "Whatever we did was too soon or too late. One almost felt ashamed to go out in Luftwaffe uniform at home." Adolf Galland wrote in his diary: "An offensive in the west was senseless. I knew that the insufficient training and lack of experience of our unit commanders meant the Jagdwaffe was doomed to failure."

For the Luftwaffe, Unternehmen Bodenplatte was its death knell. ∎

> **" Nearly out of ammunition, Rigby circled to land, but ran across another fight between a pair of P-51s and a Bf 109 "**

BLACK FRIDAY

February 9, 1945, was the darkest of days for the Royal Air Force's Coastal Command when it was tasked with finding and sinking the Z-33

WORDS: JAMIE EWAN

One wonders what went through the minds of Flt Sgt R Priest and WO J Brightwell as they pushed open the throttles of their Bristol Beaufighter TF.Xs at RAF Dallachy – just east of Elgin in Scotland's Morayshire.

It's just before 0900hrs on February 9, 1945. Assigned to No.489 Squadron Royal New Zealand Air Force, it's clear to many, maybe even them, that German shipping was on its knees – it wasn't a question of *if*, but *when* it would be defeated. But they still had a job to do. Coastal Command, which fell under the control of the Admiralty, had tasked them with a reconnaissance mission – intelligence had reported that a destroyer moving north along Norway's western coast towards Trondheim was hiding somewhere in the Vevringe Fjord. As the pair pushed northeast over the North Sea towards Norway, behind them the Dallachy Strike Wing waited.

Crossing Norway's weatherbeaten coastline about 50 miles northwest of Bergen at 1030hrs, they quickly spotted their first ship, "similar to R/boat" to quote their original report. Continuing north, they passed through the tight entrance of the ice bound Førde Fjord, only to be greeted by the immense sight of a German Narvik-class destroyer, accompanied by several other ships, including a minesweeper and a pair of flak ships, taking shelter in the fjord's tight confines and towering peaks. It was the *Z-33*, one of last remaining warships flying German colours.

Despite encountering heavy fire, the 'Beaus' continued probing numerous fjords, before turning for home around 1120hrs. As they did, they signalled their findings back, noting: "no less than five transports in Nord-Gulen, the largest between 4,000-5,000 tons, very attractive targets indeed." Almost immediately, plans to attack began. While the merchant ships were both the obvious and worthwhile targets, the Admiralty had other ideas – they wanted the destroyer. With Priest and Brightwell landing back at Dallachy around 1324hrs, by the time they walked back to operations, the first of the attacking Beaufighters were snaking their way to the runway.

Prelude to hell

By late 1944 Allied victories across France and Eastern Europe had pretty much confined German shipping to the lower waters of the Baltic and Norway. This forced Germany to use its Norwegian ports – including Bergen in the south, Trondheim in Norway's central band, and Narvik in the north – to continue the Battle of the Atlantic, move troops, and conduct trade with neutral Sweden, its primary source for much-needed iron ore. This situation wasn't helped when the Baltic iced over during the winter of 1944-1945, forcing *all* the warring nation's imports to be shipped to Narvik. With this increase in German shipping across Norwegian waters, Coastal Command transferred several anti-shipping squadrons to northern Scotland during September and October 1944 to counter them. With three de Havilland Mosquito fighter bomber squadrons (143, 235 and 248) sent to RAF Banff, about 35 miles to the west of Elgin, to form the Banff Strike Wing, four Beaufighter-equipped

BELOW: 'Wounded duck' – the wreck of Stan Butler's Beaufighter, NE831/PL-O, lies at Dallachy following the action of February 9, 1945 over the Førde Fjord. Lucky to survive their first anti-shipping strike, 13 of their colleagues never made it back.
KEY COLLECTION

ABOVE:
Dallachy Strike Wing: A mix of early and late production Bristol Beaufighter TF.Xs await their next sorties at Dallachy shortly after the strike wing was established there in late 1944. ALAMY STOCK PHOTO-PIEMAGS-WW2ARCHIVE

units arrived at Dallachy. Forming its namesake strike wing, it comprised 144 Squadron RAF, No.404 Squadron Royal Canadian Air Force, No.455 Royal Australian Air Force Squadron, and the aforementioned 489 Squadron. Their appearance quickly forced German ships travelling the Norwegian coast to sail at night and seek shelter in deep fjords during the day. Coastal Command sent near daily patrols out along the Norwegian coastline from the Skagerrak to Trondheim – often resulting in wing-sized strikes in less-than-ideal weather. To do this, they developed a gambit whereby they sent two 'outriders', piloted by experienced crews ahead to scout the countless twisting and turning fjords, to confirm the ships' locations. When it came to attacking, they had honed their tactics. Stan Butler, a 144 Squadron pilot, recalled: "These attacks required special knowledge of how to properly approach the target. The procedure we usually followed was to fly low level to the Norwegian coastline, then climb just high enough to clear the coastal mountains and head toward the selected target area. We would then commence the attack in a 'V' formation in a direction, usually east to west toward the coast, that allowed us to break off after the attack and exit directly out of the fjord. By doing this we expected the element of surprise would allow the least amount of time being spent over enemy territory and a clean get away towards the open sea before enemy fighters could be alerted and arrive on the scene."

In early 1945 it was reported the Luftwaffe had around 45 single-engined fighters based south of Trondheim – a mix of late and early variant Focke-Wulf FW 190s with Eismeergeschwader 5's 9 and 12 Staffels at Herdla near Bergen, and the Messerschmitt Bf 109G-6s and G-14s of its 10 and 11 Staffels at Gossen, about 160 miles further north. While this number barely matched the combined strength of the strike wings, many of the assigned pilots were battle-hardened veterans and aces from the Eastern Front – including Ofw Rudolf Artner and Lt Rudi Linz, who between them had already downed close to 100 Allied aeroplanes. On February 9, 1945, Staffel 9 had nine aircraft sat at

> **Despite encountering heavy fire, the 'Beaus' continued probing numerous fjords, before turning for home around 1120hrs**

BLACK FRIDAY

readiness, while 12 Staffel had three. If scrambled, they could be over the fjords of western Norway in just 20-25 minutes.

As for the Z-*33*, it had operated exclusively in Norway's frigid waters since entering frontline service in July 1943. By early 1945, it had survived everything thrown at it – including being strafed by Fleet Air Arm Corsairs IIs during Operation Mascot, the unsuccessful air raid against the German battleship *Tirpitz* in Norway's Kaafjord on July 17, 1944. On February 5, Z-*33* departed Trondheim bound for Germany. Two days later it ran aground in the shallow waters of Brufjord – the impact severely damaged the port propeller and shaft, knocked out both engines, and caused flooding. Although the crew managed to limp the vessel to Bergen that same day, they opted to return to Trondheim under the cover of darkness for repairs. Laying up in the Vevringe Fjord on February 8, she entered the Førde Fjord early the following morning – taking up residence between Mula and Heilevang. Just after 1030hrs, the valley echoed to the snarl of Priest and Brightwells' Beaufighters. Despite heavy fire, the pair escaped unscathed. Familiar with the dangers of the Norwegian coast, the Germans knew exactly what the 'Beaus' were doing and knew it was just a matter of time before a strike would arrive.

Norwegian nightmare

Within minutes of getting the signal, Wg Cdr Jack Davenport at No 18 Group RAF headquarters in Dunfermline, began planning a strike against the Z-*33*. Having previously commanded 455 Squadron, he was a veteran of such strikes. With the plan on paper, he handed it to the Dallachy Strike Wing. In turn, it was passed to Wg Cdr Colin Milson – No.455's CO. A veteran of anti-shipping operations across the Mediterranean and North Sea, the 25-year-old had reservations about what was likely to be a costly raid, especially as it was clear that hostilities were coming to an end. Despite this, he selected his crews, while his navigator, Fg Off Ralph Jones (the oldest member of the strike force at 35) plotted their route.

As they did, 12 North American Mustang IIIs of 65 Squadron were prepared for fighter escort duties, while a pair of air-sea rescue Vickers Warwick Is from 279 Squadron at nearby Fraserburgh were readied – the latter were often the only chance aircrew ditching in the North Sea had of survival. Although 12 Mustangs launched, two quickly returned home, one with engine-trouble, the other escorting it.

Canadian Bert Ramsden, a pilot officer with 404 Squadron, recalled: "We heard scuttle that a German battleship had been observed along the coast and that a couple of Beaufighters had been sent out on a reconnaissance mission. Even before confirmation was received, preparations were being made for a raid that would involve fighter-bombers from several squadrons."

As the two 'outriders' got airborne from Dallachy, nine 'Beaus' from 144 Squadron armed with four nose-mounted 20mm Hispano Mark II cannon and six wing-mounted 0.303 Browning machine guns (four starboard, two port), and 11 from both 404 and 455 Squadrons boasting the same cannon fit plus eight 60lb RP-3 rockets, followed. All were armed with a rearward facing Browning .303 operated by the navigator for defence. The crews nicknamed these the 'pop gun'.

For Stan Butler and his navigator Flt Sgt 'Nick' Nicholl in NE831/PL-O it was their first anti-shipping strike. He remembered: "Take-off was just before 1400hrs; we formed up and set course at low level in loose formation 'vics' of three. The weather was not bad; there were rain squalls here and there, but visibility was reasonably good. Everything was going according to plan." With the 'outriders' hitting the Norwegian coast west of Sognefjord, they crossed the Førde Fjord close to where the German ships had been sighted that morning – but they were nowhere to be seen.

Z-*33*'s commander, Fregattenkapitän Rudolf Menge, had opted to move further into the fjord. While several of the vessels took cover in a natural cove near Bjørkeda on the south, Z-*33* and a flak ship anchored themselves near Frammarsvik on the south side. Three more flak ships – some of which were trawlers converted for anti-aircraft

LEFT: Australian Wg Cdr Jack Davenport was instrumental in initiating the plan to attack the Z-*33*. Having previously commanded No.455 Squadron, he was a veteran of such strikes. The month before what became known as 'Black Friday', Davenport was awarded the George Medal for outstanding bravery in rescuing the pilot from the blazing cockpit of his Beaufighter after it had crash landed at RAF Langham in Norfolk. ALAMY STOCK PHOTO-PIEMAGS-WW2ARCHIVE

BELOW: A rare view of the Narvik-Class Destroyer Z-*33* steaming through Norwegian waters circa 1944. Surviving the Allied onslaught on February 9, 1945, the Z-*33* was allocated to the Soviet Union in late 1945 and turned over the falling year as the *Provornyy*. It remained in Soviet hands as a destroyer, training vessel, and later accommodation ship before a fire in 1960 resulted in it being scrapped two years later. VIA AUTHOR

> **While this number barely matched the combined strength of the strike wings, many of the assigned pilots were battle-hardened veterans and aces from the Eastern Front**

(AA) duties – positioned themselves between them. Surrounded by near vertical peaks barely a mile across at its widest point, it would be difficult to spot the ships, let alone attack them. To make matters worse, the weathered peaks and shoreline housed several AA gun batteries.

Turning east, the 'outriders' growled over the town of Førde itself, before prowling the neighbouring fjords north to south looking for any sign of the prized warship – it was still nowhere to be seen. Although they spotted a German fighter to the north and a small convoy to the south, there was no trace of the destroyer. Unbeknown to them, they had flown directly over it several times. By the time they radioed Milson at 1550hrs to report they couldn't find the ship, the FW 190s were scrambling from Herdla. With Artner taking the lead with 9 Staffel, 12 Staffel's fighters climbed above them to provide top cover. The Dallachy Strike Wing was flying into a nightmare scenario.

Into hell

With the 'outriders' job done, they turned for home. At the front of the main strike force, Milson had a hunch the destroyer was still in Førde Fjord. Pressing on from the south, the 25-year-old led them over the village of Bygstad – just eight miles from the target fjord. If the destroyer was still anchored at Heilevang, they could attack from the east, continue west through the fjord to escape into the *relative* safety of the North Sea. His watch showed it was just past 1600hrs. Butler recalled: "As we turned north with the intention of turning west into the fjord when we reached it, and making our attack 'out to sea', we suddenly found ourselves under fire from the ships... they were almost underneath us!"

Caught completely unaware as the sky erupted around them, Milson had no choice but to reposition – abandoning the attack wasn't an option. But on seeing the target, it was clear they had been expecting them and had anchored themselves in the most advantageous position. They would need to head further east to make the attack if they were to run the fjord to escape. Turning east, Milson then led the strike force south towards Førde and then west to a position just south of the fjord. Looking to the west, he soon realised that to have any chance of success, an attack out of the fjord was virtually impossible. They would have to continue west, before turning 180° to run *into* the fjord.

According to 404 Squadron's records: "...the strike wing was not prepared to attack, and the formation leader orbited the force twice to get into a suitable attack position and then ordered the attack up fjord. As [they] made their way in, they met an intense crossfire in the form of a box barrage."

With Milson attacking first, it was clear to those behind that there wasn't enough room in the fjord for more than two or three 'Beaus' at the same time. Consequently, they were queueing to make their runs. Despite heavy fire, the Beaufighters singled out their targets. According to one eyewitness: "it seemed to us it was the boats in the middle of the fjord [that] got the worst of it". Realising there was a bottleneck, some of the attacking pilots opted to come from the southwest, others from a more westerly direction – the latter using cannon and rockets against the *Z-33*. If not hit, there were certainly near-misses as it 'rocked and shaked'.

As the battle raged on, Beaufighter after Beaufighter dived into the hell below. Butler: "All this manoeuvring had taken an awfully long time. A long enough time, in fact, for enemy fighters to appear." At around 1610hrs, Plt Offs Percival Smith and Frederick 'Spike' Holly tipped in for their attack. One of 144's most experienced crews with 35 operations, this was to be their last. Diving into the fjord, Smith noticed eight dots approaching from the southwest – "Mustangs?" he mused. ▶

LEFT: Wing Commander Colin Milson was just 25 years old when he led the Dallachy Strike Wing against the German destroyer *Z-33* on February 9, 1945.
ALAMY STOCK PHOTO-PIEMAGS-WW2ARCHIVE

BELOW: August 25, 1944: This remarkable image of Beaufighters hitting a German M-Class Minesweeper off the Dutch coast captured by Fg Off Forbes Macintyre of No.455 Squadron reveals the truly chaotic nature of an anti-shipping strike. Now take this, and add the tight confines of a fjord, a near impossible to hit target, towering peaks, and enemy fighters – that's what the Dallachy Strike Wing faced on February 9, 1945...
CROWN COPYRIGHT-AIR HISTORICAL BRANCH

BLACK FRIDAY

ABOVE: This wide-angle view of the Førde Fjord on February 9, 1945 reveals the tight confines and towered peaks the Dallachy Strike Wing faced during their assault. The Z-*33* can be seen anchored among the broken ice towards the bottom of the image.
ALAMY STOCK PHOTO-HISTORY AND ART COLLECTION

Successful in their attack and evading the ships, they screamed west through the fjord to escape, while Holly surveyed the chaos behind him – as he did, he spied a fighter bearing down on them. Thinking, maybe wishing, it was a Mustang, his hopes were shattered when he saw its guns flicker. Alerting Smith over the intercom, cannon shells smashed into the cockpit and port engine. While Holly was wounded and knocked unconscious, Smith miraculously survived unscathed. Pushing his battered machine below the treetops he headed west across Naustdal. Struggling for control, he knew a forced landing was their only option. But where? This part of Norway wasn't known for being flat! Continuing west, he finally eased the machine into the ice packed waters near Høydalsfjorden – about 20 miles northwest of Førde Fjord. Quickly rescued by nearby townspeople, both men were soon captured. Seeing out the rest of the conflict as prisoners of war (POWs), Smith passed away aged 78 in December 1996, while Holly died in April 2005, aged 84.

As Smith and Holly escaped their Beau, a Mustang snarled overhead being chased by a pair of FW 190s. Suddenly diving into the valley, the Mustang appeared again below one of the '190s. Firing a short burst, it was a certain 'kill', the German fighter flicking over and crashing in a ball of flames near Solheimsstolen. The pilot was Lt Rudi Linz in his usual machine – FW 190A-8 'Blue 4' bearing his swathes of Allied 'kills' on the rudder and his wife's name, Gretel, under the cockpit. Likely dead before he crashed, he was just 27 years old.

Despite an onslaught of AA fire, 9 Staffel dove directly into the waiting Beaufighters. Ramsden: "After forming up, Milson and his formation began the attack. I was assigned to one of the following formations and due to the narrow attack area, we had to wait in a holding pattern for our turn. It was during the first attack that someone reported a small formation of planes coming from the south. Below, we could also see the German gunners must have been very experienced as they laid down a very effective blanket of flak along our approach run. A few minutes later our group commenced [its] run, but the radio chatter made it clear that at least one squadron of Luftwaffe fighters had arrived and was attacking the waiting bombers. This was very bad news as we were now more or less trapped at low level in a very narrow fjord with heavy flak coming up from below and German fighters from above. We knew our waiting bombers would be vulnerable. As usual, following our run, we were ordered to break off and head for home. As our wing guns had been replaced with rockets, we had no means of effectively fighting the Luftwaffe."

Ofw Rudolf Artner later wrote: "About 50km north of Sognefjord, we saw the enemy formation which consisted of approximately 30 Beaufighters and 10 Mustang escort fighters. During a combined attack with my Staffel, I managed to gain hits on a Beaufighter, which I attacked from behind and above. The Beaufighter crashed burning in a flat angle. The crash was noted at 1610hrs about 10km northwest of Førde. The crew did not leave the plane."

RIGHT: Armourers load RP-3s onto the wing rails of a 144 Squadron Bristol Beaufighter TF.X at Dallachy. Boasting a 60lb semi armour-piercing high-explosive warhead, this gave rise to the alternative name of the '60-pound rocket'.
ALAMY STOCK PHOTO-PIEMAGS-WW2ARCHIVE

ABOVE: Personell from No.404 Squadron RCAF pose with a Beaufighter while operating out of RAF Strubby, Lincolnshire, as part of its namesake strike wing during the summer of 1944. Ten of the men seen here were assigned to the strike against the *Z-33*. DEPARTMENT OF NATIONAL DEFENCE-ROYAL CANADIAN AIR FORCE

Possibly the first casualty of the day, it is thought this was 404 Squadron's NT922/EE-V crewed by Canadian Plt Offs William Jackson, 27, and his navigator William Blunderfield – aged just 22. Both were killed. Within minutes, another four of the unit's Beaufighters had fallen, including NT890/EE-F with Fg Offs Charles Smerneos (24) and Norman Cochrane (25), NE761/EE-W with Fg Off Philip Myrick (22) and Plt Off Claude Berges (27), and RD136/EO-Q1 with Fg Off Harry Smook (20) and Plt Off Alan Duckworth (23). They were all killed.

Artner gained his second claim of the day not far from where Linz fell – barely three minutes after the first. It was his 19th 'kill'. Of it, he wrote: "I managed to hit another Beaufighter twice during a low-level chase. The plane finally turned and crashed straight into the ground after yet another salvo. The crash was noted at 1613hrs about 5km north-northwest of Naustdal."

It's not known which Beaufighter this was – but 455 Squadron also lost two aircraft that day: NV199/UB-O, crewed by Flt Lt Robert McColl and WO Arthur MacDonald who survived to become POWs, and NV196/UB-V crewed by WO Donald Mutimer and Plt Off John Blackshaw – both were killed. Like many of the Beaufighters lost that day, the precise cause may never be established. It's a similar story for one seen to crash into a swamp and burst into flames near Naustdol. Although locals tried in vain to save the crew, their efforts were beaten by the intense heat and exploding ammunition. This may have been one of the crews from 404 Squadron, locals reportedly hearing German soldiers saying "Arme Kanadier".

LEFT: This image captured from a No.455 Squadron RAAF machine shows the *Z-33* under attack on February 9, 1945. Eyewitnesses recalled the ship 'rocked and shaked' under the onslaught of fire from the Dallachy Beaufighters. ALAMY STOCK PHOTO-HISTORY AND ART COLLECTION

They fell in all directions...

Leading in Mustang KH788/YQ-T, Flt Lt Jonnie Foster spotted the swarm of German fighters. Watching as they pounced on the unsuspecting Beaufighters orbiting Vevring, Foster alerted the others. As he did so, the FW 190s of 12 Staffel appeared heading directly for him. Managing to fire a short burst at one before diving away, he saw several hits around its engine before it spewed a trail of black smoke. Later identified as Lt Karl-Heinz 'Charly' Koch's FW 190A-8 'Blue 9', the five-victory ace escaped the stricken machine just before it crashed into the sea near Heilevang.

Another Mustang claimed Fj Ofw Otto Leibfried's FW 190 ('White 22', an F-8 fighter-bomber) near Gjesneset – the pilot noting "hits in the cockpit, wings, and engine" before it was "engulfed in flames". Although wounded, Leibfried managed to bale out, but landed in the treacherous terrain of the nearby peaks. It was reported that "in the nights following the battle, people could see his flares calling for assistance, but there was little the Norwegian or German patrols could do." His body was found later that year.

As the battle developed into a whirling maelstrom of FW 190s, Mustangs, and Beaufighters, aircraft fell in all directions. Near Gaular, residents saw an FW 190 ('White 1' piloted by Uffz Heinz Orlowski) chase down a 'Beau'. Hit several times, the pilot attempted to crash land, but the rising terrain made it impossible. Hitting the hillside with a sickening ▶

BLACK FRIDAY

crash, horrified witnesses saw the Beaufighter "break in half" and "the cockpit-section slide down the hillside". Later identified as No 404's NV422/EE-C flown by Fg Offs Hugh Lynch and Oswald Knight, both men were killed. Aged 24 and 27, they had joined the squadron just three weeks before. This was their first strike.

Seeing that Beaufighter in trouble, WO Cecil Caesar gave chase in Mustang HB836/YT-N. Pursuing the German fighter, a low-level duel developed. Suddenly catching fire, the Mustang entered a wide turn. It will never be known what happened in the cockpit of the American-built fighter — to some it looked like Caesar was trying to get away, to others he was trying to crash land. Despite his aeroplane burning fiercely, he never attempted to bale out. Instead, he turned back into the fight, before "ploughing" into the pine forest below like a "burning torch". The sole Mustang lost; Caesar was killed. But it wasn't in vain — Orlowski was forced to bale out moments later, his FW 190's engine had been damaged during the skirmish. Escaping from the cockpit at very low level, he was too close to the ground for his 'chute to open. Crashing into the snow-clad hillside, he miraculously survived, unhurt. Incredibly, his only injuries were sustained when a small avalanche carried him down the valley — his flare gun went off resulting in severe burns on one leg. He spent the rest of the war convalescing.

Fighting back

Despite knowing their Beaufighters were no match for the FW 190s, the Dallachy Wing threw themselves into the battle — including Fg Off J Nelson and WO R Gracie of 404 Squadron in NT916/EO-S. Seeing a 'Beau' being hounded by a pair of '190s, they gave chase, shooting one down. With the other turning into them, Gracie managed to hit it with a burst from his 'pop gun'. It quickly flew away. For "driving a 190 off a comrade's tail" Nelson was awarded the DFC. Another 'Beau' (NE686/EO-T, crewed by Fg Off H Flynn and Plt Off M Michael) engaged a pair of '190s, but lost them in the whirling mass of aeroplanes. It's hard to imagine the scenes in the Beaufighters as the crews fought to survive while trying to avoid each other, the anti-aircraft fire, enemy fighters, and the valley walls. They nevertheless continued to press home their attacks, seemingly with disregard to the immense peril. One witness recalled watching gunners on the ships fall under the return fire from the Beaufighters, only to be replaced by new ones — such was the intensity of the battle.

Spotting the Z-33 among the melee, Flynn unleashed his rockets. He was credited with two RP strikes. On his right wing was NT922/EE-V with William Jackson and William Blunderfield who were lost moments later — it's not known if they hit their intended target. Flynn's 'number two' was Canadian Fg Off Roger Savard and his navigator Plt Off Jeffery Middleton in NV292/EE-O. Both men were approaching the end of their tour. Diving through the onslaught,

RIGHT: The ferocity of a Beaufighter attack is evident in this view of the German flak ship 'Mosel' under fire from aircraft from No.404 Squadron machines off the coast of Norway on October 15, 1944. The Beaufighter visible on the right is NV422/EE-C, which was lost with its crew (Fg Offs Hugh Lynch and Oswald Knight) during the attack on the Z-33. ALAMY STOCK PHOTO-PIEMAGS-WW2ARCHIVE

BELOW: One of the flak ships – likely a fishing trawler converted for anti-aircraft duties – accompanying the Z-33 bears the brunt of a 'Beau' attack on February 9, 1945. ALAMY STOCK PHOTO-HISTORY AND ART COLLECTION

their Beaufighter was peppered by AA fire — severely injuring Middleton. Their aircraft ablaze, Savard successfully crash landed on the ice. Although they survived the initial impact, NV292 flipped onto its back — trapping both. With Norwegian civilians rushing to help them, they were soon forced to retreat when German soldiers fired on them. Witnesses later saw both being freed by German flak crews, but by then Middleton, 30, had succumbed to his wounds. Savard spent the rest of the war as a prisoner.

"Weave, for Christ's sake!"

The last Beaufighter to attack was Stan Butler's. Seeing two smaller vessels, he lined up on the one that was "easiest to get at". He recalled: "We got in quite a long burst, bang on target. Hypnotising for a first timer, so hypnotising that there was a danger of not pulling out of your dive in time! We flattened out. Nick saw a ship's mast flash past and then, on our port, the destroyer tucked close into the fjord wall. It seemed to be only yards away and was giving us a continuous broadside with everything it had as we jinked along its length. Being last into the attack, and probably their only remaining target, we were getting plenty of unwelcome attention. It was a frightening moment."

While trying to escape the inferno, a small calibre round smashed into the cockpit. Miraculously, both men were unhurt – but it destroyed a distribution manifold in the hydraulic system at the base of Butler's control column. Manoeuvring wildly to spoil the AA gunners' aim, hydraulic fluid splashed over them and the canopy – killing their visibility. Suddenly, Nicholl discovered "the unmistakable front silhouette of an FW 190 with little lights sparkling along its wings". Shouting "Weave, for Christ's sake! Weave, weave!" as a burst of tracer flashed by, Butler threw the 'Beau' around the sky. With Nicholl firing a red Very flare to alert the fighter escort, a Mustang soon chased off the offending Focke-Wulf as they continued into the Førde Fjord looking for somewhere to escape its cavernous walls, the rugged ridgeline hiding in the clouds above them.

Although damaged, their aircraft was still flying – and they were still alive. Behind them, burning wreckage marked the spots where men, many younger than the author is now, lost their lives. Setting course for home, they negotiated the North Sea, before Dallachy appeared in front of them – a sight to behold. Unaware of the true extent of their damage, they opted for a wheels-up landing. Butler said: "Out of the corners of my eyes, I was fascinated to see the props stop – the starboard first, and then… wallop – we hit the deck. I vividly recall pressing hard on the brakes, but I had no wheels!" Another 'Beau' landing wheels up at Dallachy was 455 Squadron's NE798/UB-Q piloted by Fg Off C Thompson and his navigator WO I Gordon.

With almost 50 aeroplanes involved, the battle over the Førde Fjord was, and still is, the

LEFT:
Uffz Heinz Orlowski was one of the pilots from Eismeergeschwader 5's 9 Staffel scrambling from Herdla on February 9, 1945. Piloting FW 190F-8 'White 1', he was forced to bale out following a low-level duel with 65 Squadron's WO Cecil Caesar – the latter's final act of war. By the time Orlowski escaped his battered machine, Caesar was dead. VIA AUTHOR

BLACK FRIDAY

RIGHT: Incredibly, Orlowski's FW 190F-8 'White 1' (Werk Nummer 931862) was salvaged in September 1983 and has since been restored to flying condition as N91FW by GossHawk Unlimited in Arizona for its owner – the Massachusetts-based Collings Foundation. It is seen here undertaking its first engine run on January 31, 2023 – almost 78 years to the day that the former Luftwaffe fighter was shot down over Norway. In 2005 Orlowski visited it and sat in his fighter once more. He died in 2010. GOSSHAWK UNLIMITED-LINDSEY GOSS

largest air combat ever to have taken place over Norway. The entire battle was over by 1630hrs – less than 15 minutes after it had started. With the surviving Beaufighter crews breaking for home, many of them injured and fighting to keep their damaged aeroplanes in the air, the FW 190s landed at Herdla at 1655hrs – barely an hour after scrambling. The last Beaufighter landed at Dallachy at 1845hrs. That aircraft was No.455's NV450/UB-X piloted by Fg Off H Spink and his navigator Fg Off O L Clifford. Despite both crew being wounded, Spink severely, the pair had managed to limp home. There, they made a wheels-up landing in the dark – an incredible feat in view of the damage to both them and their aircraft. Both received the DFC. Although they waited for more to arrive, they knew the effort was in vain.

One of those watching them return was Andrew Hendrie. Then stationed at Dallachy, he later went on to author numerous books on the efforts, struggles, and sacrifices of Coastal Command during World War Two. He recalled: "They landed like a flight of wounded ducks... a number just pancaking. It was like a Hollywood film set – but this was real. Later in the mess I saw some of the Beaufighter aircrew with their clothing truly in ribbons."

Of the 31 Beaufighters despatched, eight were lost – killing 13 men, the other five becoming POWs. Six of those lost belonged to 404 Squadron. Hendrie added: "In the mess about that time, I heard broadcast Elgar's 'Chanson de Matin', music ever to recall in my mind 404 Squadron's 'Black Friday'." In his logbook entry Ramsden wrote: "Black Friday. Six of 11 lost" alongside a sombre list of their nicknames. In the unit's Operations Record Book for February 9, 1945, the adjutant, Flt Lt 'Wilkie' Wilkinson penned: "Today's losses were a staggering blow, and a keen sense of personal loss is felt by every member of the squadron and the servicing echelon."

As for the *Z-33* and its escort, the damage was classed as light – despite the destroyer suffering an explosion following a successful hit by Flt Lt J Powers of 144 Squadron, and a minesweeper being set alight. With none of the ships sunk, Coastal Command's darkest day was made that bit worse when it was revealed that ULTRA – British military intelligence – was already aware that the *Z-33* was located where she was. Such is the way of war. ■

RIGHT: Today, the remnants of the BMW 801 engine belonging to Lt Rudi Linz's FW 190-A8 'Blue 4' (Werk Nummer 732183) survives in the Luftkampmuseet (Air Battle Museum) at Naustdal – just three miles or so from where the *Z-33* was anchored that fateful day. ALAMY STOCK PHOTO-PETER HOLLY